EARTHKEEPERS ™

**Four keys for helping young people
live in harmony with the earth**

by
Steve Van Matre
and Bruce Johnson

Designed and Produced by
The Institute for Earth Education

Cover by Jan Muir
Additional art by Jan Muir,
Matt Haag, Sarah Rowlatt,
Pat Buchtel and Dave Wampler

Typesetting and Layout by
The Calgary Board of Education

First Printing, June 1988

ISBN: 0-917011-01-5

Library of Congress: 87-82847

Published by

The Institute for Earth Education
Box 288, Warrenville, Illinois 60555 U.S.A.

Printed in the United States

Dedication

To the
environmental education and interpretation
graduate students from
George Williams College
and
Aurora University
whose patience and perseverance
have contributed so much to
the development of our
earth education programs

TABLE OF CONTENTS

ACKNOWLEDGEMENTS

We're often asked in the institute how we develop these programs, especially since we have no full-time staff nor outside sources of funding. Since we consider such work to be just about the most important thing we do, we pay special attention to training and preparing some of our Associate members to become more involved with us in this way. Generally, it takes several years before our volunteer staff members are able to participate fully in the capacity of a program designer, but when they are ready, their commitment and dedication produces programs like this one.

The creation of the Earthkeepers program was prompted by the staff of the McKeever Environmental Learning Center in Sandy Lake, Pennsylvania. They wanted a shorter earth education program to offer those schools who could not participate in our longer Sunship Earth program, which they had been conducting for several years. At the request of the center, we put a program development team together for Earthkeepers in 1983. Fortunately, the team was able to begin by drawing upon some Conceptual Encounters the institute had previously developed for the Florida State Parks under the leadership of our Regional Coordinator in that area, Dick Roberts. Using those concept-building activities as a starting point gave the team a tremendous boost in their initial efforts. (Much appreciation should also go here to Eddie Soloway who coordinated our program development work for that original Florida project.)

The primary members of the Earthkeepers development team, in addition to the authors, were Fran Bires and Mike Mayer. They provided the beginning coordination for the Earthkeepers undertaking, and thus deserve the thanks of all those who use this program. Fran Bires also played a significant role in his ongoing participation in the piloting phases of our developmental approach. From the beginning Fran has been willing to undertake every conceivable last minute change dreamed up in furtherance of an improved outcome for his learners. It's not often that one finds leaders in our field as willing as Mike and Fran were to commit themselves so quickly to the problems and pressures and permutations of such an undertaking.

Once our formal piloting got underway, another one of our Regional Coordinators came to our aid as well. Rich Horton raised some much-needed funding for us through his center, Shaker Lakes Regional Nature Center, and hired the institute's program coordinator, Bruce Johnson, to implement the program at Rich's center in Cleveland, Ohio. A bit later, our Coordinator for Canada, Ron Sweet, made it possible for the Calgary Board of Education to also become a primary sponsor through its Outdoor Schools Program. Without the combined support provided by Rich Horton and Ron Sweet, Earthkeepers would certainly have taken much longer to complete and probably would not have turned out as nicely.

During the last piloting phase, our Associates at the Shaw Arboretum in Missouri, Greg Krone and Gary Schimmelpfenig, came up with some additional support in their budget, and Martin Bragg at The Wilderness Centre in England was able to trial the activities and give us a British perspective on their effectiveness. Much credit must go to all these folks and their respective institutions for our success in putting this program together.

A sincere thanks must also go to the teachers, students and parents who have participated in our pilots. Their reactions, comments and critiques have been an important part of the Earthkeepers development process. The following schools participated in the Earthkeepers pilot:

Shaker Heights, Ohio
  Fernway, Moreland, Sussex,
  Onaway, Boulevard, Mercer and
  Lomond Schools
Cleveland Heights/University
Heights, Ohio
  Roxboro Elementary, Coventry,
  Belvoir, Canterbury, Noble,
  Boulevard, Fairfax and Oxford
  Schools
St. Louis, Missouri
  Concord Lutheran, Carr-Lane,
  Meramec Elementary, New City,
  Wilson and Principia Schools
St. Charles, Missouri
  Null School
University City, Missouri
  Delmar-Harvard School
Indiana, Pennsylvania
  Ben Franklin, Horace Mann and
  Eisenhower Schools
Erie, Pennsylvania
  Grandview, Greene and
  Vernondale Schools
Sharon, Pennsylvania
  Case Avenue and Sharon Gifted
  Schools
Pittsburgh, Pennsylvania
  Fox Chapel Country Day, Marzolf,
  St. Benedict the Moor and Holy
  Rosary Schools
Mars, Pennsylvania
  Haine and Rowan Schools
Baden, Pennsylvania
  Mt. Gallitzin Academy
Saegertown, Pennsylvania
  Saegertown Middle School
Saltsburg, Pennsylvania
  Saltsburg Elementary School
Blairsville, Pennsylvania
  Burrell and Third Ward Schools
Strattanville, Pennsylvania
  Clarion Limestone Elementary
  School

Zelionople, Pennsylvania
  Connoquenessing Valley
  Elementary School
Evans City, Pennsylvania
  Evans City Elementary School
Farrell, Pennsylvania
  Farrell Gifted School
North East, Pennsylvania
  Greenfield Elementary School
Hermitage, Pennsylvania
  Hermitage Gifted School
Homer City, Pennsylvania
  Homer Center
Jamestown, Pennsylvania
  Jamestown Elementary School
Mercer Pennsylvania
  Mercer Area Elementary School
West Sunbury, Pennsylvania
  Moniteau School District
West Middlesex, Pennsylvania
  Oakview Middle School
Calgary, Alberta
  Keeler, Rundle, Richmond,
  Rosedale, Currie, Haysboro,
  Jeannie Elliot, Erin Woods and
  W.O.Mitchell Elementary Schools
Chipping Campden, Gloucestershire
  The Federated Schools of Ebrington
  & St. James
Gloucester, Gloucestershire
  Highnam Church of England
  Primary School
Cheltenham, Gloucestershire
  Elmbridge Junior School
Lydbrook County, Gloucestershire
  Lydbrook County Primary School
Cinderford, Gloucestershire
  Latimer Junior School
  St. Whites County Primary School

Several other Associate members of the institute's volunteer staff also played important roles in the Earthkeepers effort. They deserve a special thanks for their extra work in supporting the completion of this material.

Gary Rasberry	Deb Lyons
Eddie Soloway	Dave Wampler
Mike Kerry	

In addition, the following people have contributed directly to the development of the Earthkeepers program (an asterisk indicates institute members):

Laurie Farber*	Deb Merriam*
Ellen Goldberg	Nancy Bires*
Roger Tucker*	Marilyn Coker*
Bill Weiler*	Kirk Hoessle*
Lorna Way*	Matthew Daw*
Jeff McFadden*	Rob Pegg
John Lyons*	Roxanna Heidbrier
Robert Schuh*	Bill Coutts*
Dan Best	Margaret Johnson
Bill Prime*	Ethel Lumby

Once again, we're indebted to Jan Muir* for her artwork, which brings many of the words herein to life. This time Jan was ably aided by Matt Haag* who illustrated the Conceptual Encounters, Sarah Rowlatt who illustrated the speck trail guidebook pages and Pat Buchtel who drew the Time Capsules murals. And thanks to the interpretive design firm of Sycamore Associates who produced the slide show for our opening activity under a contract with Shaker Lakes Regional Nature Center. (Jan coordinated that project as well.)

We were very fortunate to have been able to use the abilities of the Calgary Board of Education's Physical and Outdoor Education Team and Media Production Department to prepare the Earthkeepers materials for publication. Special thanks to Penny Dowswell, Kathleen McCallum and especially Brad Wonnacott, Cathy Giroux and Ron Sweet, for their efforts in this area.

In the end much of the credit for this manual should also go to a group of students in the environmental education program development course at Aurora University. They prepared the early drafts of several important pieces here. In particular, the help of the following students proved invaluable in adding some direction and momentum to this part of the project:

Dave White*   Vicki Onderdonk
Steve Barg*   Dave Falvo

Finally, thanks to all of our members around the world for their continuing support – a portion of each of their annual contributions went towards our program development effort.

THE INSTITUTE FOR EARTH EDUCATION

"Learning to Live Lightly"

The Institute for Earth Education is a nonprofit volunteer organization made up of an international network of individuals and member organizations. We believe that a special kind of education – EARTH EDUCATION – can make a significant difference in the health of our planet. Earth Education is the process of helping people build an understanding of, appreciation for, and harmony with the earth and its life. All our activities and programs are designed to help achieve this goal.

Originally known as the Acclimatization Institute, our work builds on the pioneering efforts documented in the <u>Acclimatization</u> and <u>Acclimatizing</u> books. However, since their publication in the early seventies, we have learned that a few environmental activities are not enough. There remains an urgent need for complete educational programs – programs that focus primarily on understanding basic ecological systems (such as, energy flow, cycling, and interrelationships), what these systems mean for people in their own lives, and what people must do to begin living more in harmony with these systems which support all life on earth. Today, The Institute for Earth Education has branches underway in the United States, Canada, Britain, France, and Australia.

The major work of the institute is to design and develop specific educational programs that change people's view of our home, the planet earth, and the way they interact with it. Sunship Earth, our first complete program (designed for upper elementary students), has achieved widespread attention since it first appeared in 1980. Outdoor Leaders around the world have called it the most focussed, innovative and hard-hitting environmental education program ever produced.

We're the Practitioners

How are we different from other environmental groups? No other organization in this field exists solely to develop and disseminate quality educational programs. True, lots of groups have created activities to sprinkle around, but we're creating complete programs. Lots of groups serve as umbrella organizations for those with a wide range of interests and intentions, but we're chartered for those primarily interested in the educational process. Lots of groups are working on the present problems, but we're preparing people to deal with the future ones. We believe strong, focussed educational programs serve as a seedbed for the advocacy necessary to preserve this fascinating planet we share.

We believe:
- Earth education should be a separate and distinct part of every school curriculum, youth program and adult organization.
- Understanding basic ecological concepts (and their meaning in our daily lives) is too important to leave to a chance lesson or activity or talk.
- Heightened feelings for the natural world combined with increased understandings about its systems form the foundation for positive environmental action.
- All programs should require their participants to begin making personal improvements in their own environmental habits, while insuring that their leaders and sites serve as models themselves.
- Earth Education is a serious task, but getting to know the earth should be a lifelong adventure full of wonder and joy.

If you share such beliefs, please contact us for a packet of membership information. We think you'll find many kindred spirits in our growing earth education family.

INTRODUCTION

Since the publication of <u>Sunship Earth</u> in 1979, we've listened to hundreds of teachers and leaders engaged in running that program, collected our own observations from dozens of Sunship Earth Stations in several countries, and corresponded with countless folks who were already involved with us or just interested in setting up a program of their own.

In fact, one of the nice things about our work is that when you get involved in earth education you are essentially tying into a worldwide network of people offering the same programs, trying to solve the same problems. We believe we are the only educational group in this field that can offer that kind of help and support and perspective.

In the end, all those comments and observations boiled down to a short list of requirements that became the design criteria for our Earthkeepers program:

- ○ less time
- ○ less leaders
- ○ less dependence on fair weather
- ○ less props
- ○ more transfer
- ○ more help with the tools and props

As you will see, Earthkeepers meets almost all of these

criteria. It takes only 2½ days. Two people can run it. It can be offered in any season, and over half of the program must be completed back in the classroom.

Unfortunately, we didn't do as well with the props. Although the program requires less of these learning helpers than Sunship Earth, there are still a fair amount of them. However, as anyone can attest who has ever worked on designing a program, the problem arises when you try to take large ecological concepts that exist primarily as abstractions at any one point in time and space, and turn them into focussed, stimulating, concrete, participatory learning experiences in the here and how. Sure, it's easy to get your hands on a piece of the water cycle, for example, but how do you get the whole thing – the largest physical process on earth – into the concrete? Doing that without props is almost impossible. Nonetheless, we have tried to make it a bit easier this time, and the institute plans to supply more of the tools and materials needed itself.

Supplemental and Infusion = Superficial and Ineffective

Before I get into this next section, let me say, right off, we don't think we have all the answers in this field; in fact, we're sure of it. That's why we encourage people to build their own earth education programs, in their own settings and situations. Unfortunately, the usual approach in our field has been to provide teachers and leaders with a collection of activities along with the caveat to use them in any way they see fit. As a result, most of the environmental education activities that have been developed are merely sprinkled, like so much spice, over a melange of other educational pursuits. They seldom lead one into developing a complete, integrated educational program with real behavioural change in mind. To put it bluntly, the point of environmental education should be change. If there is no change, there is no point. Our field desperately needs more leaders who are willing to work for the kind of focussed learning that will effect actual change in people's daily live.

Naturally, we hope lots of places in pursuit of this goal will elect to set up the entire 2½ day Earthkeepers program that uses our activities, but for those who cannot, we still want to encourage them to use our work to build a complete program.

From the very beginning those of us in the institute have taken a programmatic focus, i.e., we've emphasized creating specific learning programs instead of supplemental activities. (Even Acclimatizing, although often viewed differently in the field, was seen by us as an extension of the original six-hour Acclimatization program.) We've always been extremely suspicious of the claim that the way to produce environmentally responsible citizens is to merely infuse the school curriculum with environmental messages. And after almost twenty years of listening to people talk about such an approach, we've yet to find anyone who has done it anyway. Oh, there are some packages of activities and miscellaneous guides still in print, but no genuine, integrated curriculum has ever emerged.

On the other hand, a learning program, as opposed to the usual collection of supplemental learning activities, is a carefully-crafted series of focussed, cumulative learning experiences designed with specific outcomes in mind. It doesn't matter if it's a program to learn how to read, how to play tennis, how to speak another language, how to drive a car or how to live more lightly on the earth. The fundamental nature of all instructional programs is the same. Of course, if it's a good program, it is also probably interactive and dynamic. It captures the learners' attention, pulls them into its experiences and gives them something to do with what happens to them.

The "supplementalists" are fond of saying that their goal is to teach students how to think, not what to think. Our goal is to teach students why and how to live more lightly on the earth, and to help them develop a deeper personal relationship with it.

Tomorrow's Answer Today

Naturally, there's been a price to pay for our intransigence about all this, but in all good conscience we cannot keep silent. Our response has been to develop a two-pronged approach: on the one hand we've forged ahead on developing and implementing genuine programs, magical and meaningful educational adventures that captivate both learners and leaders alike, and at the same time, we've continued to challenge the supplemental, infusion model that dominates our field.

We remain convinced that it's not enough to sprinkle a few environmental lessons around, and that a couple of outside activities, a poster on the bulletin board and a litter pick-up campaign in the spring do not a program make. We believe that the most pressing need in the educational portion of the environmental movement is to reach out to those leaders and teachers who are ready for something more and let them know there's an alternative.

○ They don't have to rely on traditionally boring identification walks, or nature crafts, or worksheets and discussions to fulfill environmental education requirements.

○ They don't have to use reworked "New Games" or science experiments to try to teach ecological understandings.

○ They don't have to talk about environmental problems on a field trip, then return to energy intense and consumptive classrooms.

○ They don't have to push their students into getting in touch with the natural world and caring about what it means in their own lives.

○ They don't have to feel isolated and alone, surrounded by those who neither yearn for quality programs, nor understand the real causes of our environmental crisis.

We believe Earthkeepers represents an important option. However, it is not a culmination unit. It serves as a dynamic, 2½ day springboard for what can take place back at school. Nor is it meant to be a panacea for what ails us in environmental education. Earthkeepers provides a framework on which the teacher must continue building. Apprentice Earthkeepers return to school:

○ motivated to carry on with their learning

○ possessing the tools and plans for the next phase of their work

○ understanding the essential idea of some basic ecological processes

○ feeling better about the natural world and their relationship with it

○ aware of the possibility of future rewards for their efforts

○ knowing some things they can do personally to help solve our environmental problems

Instead of sprinkling a few activities and messages around at random, the teacher returns with a carefully-crafted framework on which to build and a classroom full of willing, enthusiastic carpenters. Together, they can begin examining their own actions in their own settings and start crafting lifestyles that have less impact upon the earth.

Remember, when it comes to our environmental crisis, they are not the problem, we are.

E.M. is with you,

S.V.M.
Stratford-upon-Avon
May, 1987

THE WHYS, WHATS AND WAYS
OF EARTH EDUCATION

Before we begin examining the structure of earth education, perhaps we should first answer the question why we are calling our work earth education now instead of environmental education. Frankly, we've given up on the original term. Here are some excerpts from "Environmental Education: Mission Gone Astray", a speech we offer to conferences and centers to encourage their leaders to rethink their viewpoints about this urgent educational work:

> Have you ever noticed that the simplest things in life are often the hardest to say? Things like - "I love you," "I believe," "Yes," "I'm sorry".... Well, I have a problem like that. I'm working on a new book called Earth Education: A New Beginning, and to be honest, I'm having a lot of trouble with my opening line. How do you say you're sorry, and sound like you mean it, in advance? How do you apologize to those your words may offend even before you say them? How do you adequately explain that you are not attacking the people, but challenging the state of our field?
>
> You see, we think environmental education has gone astray – not because we lack money or facilities or volunteers – but because we've lost a clear sense of our direction and our mission. And my fear is that any

criticisms will sound like we're belittling everything and everyone, or come across like we have all the answers. We're not, and we don't....

However, poke your head into most any school today and see how much real environmental education you find going on there. I don't mean a couple of activities (inside or out) led by one or two valiant teachers, I mean **focussed**, **sequential**, instructional **programs** as a regular, integral part of the whole curriculum. Not much luck? Try the teachers' closets. That's where you'll probably find the most evidence. Look for the now unused books, boxes, pouches and kits that were once common to our field, plus the obligatory mimeographed curriculum guide. Chances are good that most of it gets very little use these days.

And if a few teachers do include an environmental lesson or unit, chances are good that they do not systematically address what environmental education set out in the beginning to accomplish, i.e., how life functions ecologically, what that means for people in their own lives, and what they are going to have to do to change their lifestyles in order to lessen their impact upon the earth.

Next, stop by your average nature center or outdoor school and see what you find there as well. The name of the place may have changed, but the staff is probably back to identifying the plants, doing tombstone rubbings, taking Ph tests, reading the weather gauges, making maple syrup, etc. In other words, they're probably offering a loose assemblage of outside activities (yes, with some sensory awareness experiences from Acclimatization and a few similar environmental games thrown in) all tied together by a schedule rather than a desire to achieve particular learning outcomes.

After you've made the rounds of our educational institutions, sit down and sift through some of the major so-called environmental education programs that were developed. You're in for a surprise. You'll find that several of them didn't even deal with basic ecological understandings, i.e., concepts like energy flow or cycling or diversity. You're asking, "How could someone possibly claim to have a comprehensive environmental education program and not deal directly and effectively with the fundamental basis for all life on the planet – the flow of sunlight energy?" That's a good question. What's amazing is that its been so seldom asked.

Other projects, as you'll see, dealt with some of the concepts, but never attempted to clarify for their participants how their lives were connected to those concepts, nor suggested that they should examine their lifestyles in light of their new understandings. A couple of projects included a framework, even placed ecological understanding within it, but then provided only a disjointed, random accumulation of not very stimulating activities to get the job done that they had so carefully identified in their organizational structure. As a result, you often got either the activities with no good framework, or the framework with no good activities.

It's also going to be pretty obvious in your examination that for some of these projects their activities were created first and their objectives formulated later. In fact, chances are good that any time you find an activity description that claims to accomplish several objectives simultaneously, then you've found an activity that was not developed with a specific learning outcome in mind. Instead, someone probably got a group together to come up with things to do, then figured out what their products were really going to achieve afterwards.

You should also check out how they placed such activities in various subject areas while you're at it. It probably went something like this – imagine for a moment people sitting around a table commenting upon an activity like making maple syrup: "Well, let's see, they figured out the number of buckets of sap it takes to make a jar of syrup didn't they, so it's a math activity." "Ok. And they listened to the sap gurgling beneath the bark, that means it's a science activity." "Don't forget when we told them how the pioneers did it. That's

social studies." "True, and they had to write a report on it when they got back, so it fits in language arts as well." Want to guess how someone would justify this as an environmental education activity to begin with? "Well, we discussed multiple forest roles with the kids while they watched the sap boiling down." R-i-g-h-t....

Perhaps the most damaging development though was the assertion you'll find in many of these projects that leaders should use the materials in any way they like. In other words, people should just pick and choose whatever caught their fancy, or whatever happened to fit with what they were doing at the time. Hardly anyone said, "Hey folks, if you're going to be serious about the task of environmental education, then it won't work just to sprinkle a couple of activities around like so much spice. You're going to have to put together some focussed, sequential programs to get the job done. Just bagging up a batch of activities and calling them a program is like tape recording a batch of sounds and calling them a symphony...."

In the end, I think we're going to have to face up to it: a lot of otherwise well-meaning people have been misled about the nature and purpose of environmental education. And as a result its become everything to everyone, and not much of anything to anyone. One of my favorite definitions that appeared in the early days was the one that goes "environmental education is education that is in, about, or for the environment." Gosh, no wonder people got confused. Under that definition, what isn't environmental education? And if any of these perplexed folks went off to a national conference looking for some answers, they would probably find everything from orienteering to acid rain on the program. Or in other words, everything from outdoor recreation to environmental studies. It's no wonder that the idea of developing focussed, comprehensive education programs seemed to get lost in all of this jumbled potpourri of goals and offerings.

Here's the bottom line: we don't need collections of supplemental curriculum activities. They won't get the job done. We need specific, comprehensive units of instruction for specific settings and situations. Let's develop these focussed programs and then go out there and sell them to the boards of education, youth groups, nature centers, adult organizations, park districts, etc. Anything short of this will only further the educational hypocrisy that already exists. Please don't misunderstand: we don't think our way is the only way to get there, but we do think knowing where we're going and paying attention to how people learn is a big advantage. Nor do we think that everyone should be doing earth education all of the time, but we do think its influence on everything else is inescapable. Finally, we don't mean to belittle everything that's been done in the past, but we do think that many of those in pursuit of E.E. have lost their way.

Again, I apologize for how negative all this sounds, but I think it was Einstein who said, "If you don't know there's a problem, you don't have anything to think about." Believe me, there's a problem. Won't you join us in thinking about it?

-Steve Van Matre

Okay. So we're starting over....

Earth Education is the process of helping people live more harmoniously and joyously with the natural world. And we have divided the overall structure of that process into three parts: the Whys, the Whats, and the Ways. Each of the three combine to form the supporting pyramid for the process of helping others build an understanding of, appreciation for, and harmony with the earth and its life.

Why Earth Education? Simply because the human passengers on board the planet earth are endangering most other living things that share the planet with them and their own life support systems in the process. Today, earth advocates are desperately needed to serve as teachers and models and to champion the existence of our fellow non-human passengers. We also believe that people who have broader understandings and deeper feelings for the planet as a vessel of life are wiser and healthier and happier themselves.

What Does It Include? Understanding, feeling and processing are the key components of the earth education edifice. In order to live more in harmony with other life on our planet, people first need a basic understanding of its ecological systems and communities. Next, they must feel a deep and abiding emotional attachment to all life. And finally, they must begin processing their new understandings and feelings by making changes in their own lifestyles.

How Is It Accomplished? First, careful structuring provides the framework for creating complete programs with adventuresome, magical learning experiences that focus on specific outcomes. Second, earth education immerses its participants in lots of rich, firsthand contact with the natural world. And third, relating these experiences to their own lives is encouraged by providing individuals with time to be alone in natural settings where they can reflect upon both the other life around them and their own actions.

THE WHYS

preserving

We believe the earth as we know it is endangered by its human passengers.

nurturing

We believe people who have broader understandings and deeper feelings for the planet as a vessel of life are wiser and healthier and happier.

training

We believe earth advocates are needed to serve as environmental teachers and models, and to champion the existence of earth's nonhuman passengers.

THE WHATS

understanding

We believe in developing in people a basic comprehension of the major ecological systems and communities of the planet.

feeling

We believe in instilling in people deep and abiding emotional attachments to the earth and its life.

processing

We believe in preparing people to live more harmoniously and joyously with the earth and all its passengers.

THE WAYS

structuring

We believe in building complete programs with adventuresome, magical learning experiences that focus on specific outcomes.

immersing

We believe in including lots of rich, firsthand contact with the natural world.

relating

We believe in providing individuals with time to be alone in natural settings where they can reflect upon all life.

Earth Education Programs

An Earth Education program is a skillfully crafted, sequential learning experience designed to help participants live more harmoniously and joyously with the earth and all its life.

We believe a learning program, as opposed to a collection of randomly strung together, dissimilar activities, is more focussed on and committed to its outcomes. A good program provides the intrinsic motivation necessary to pull the learners into a sequence of cumulative activities designed to achieve an overall objective. It involves the learners in interactive and dynamic ways. And in the end, it is synergistic – all the pieces interact together in such a way that the whole becomes more than the sum of its parts.

Gathering up a bunch of unrelated activities and calling them a program is like recording a batch of unrelated sounds and calling them a symphony. We strive to make an Earth Education program a carefully crafted symphony on living more harmoniously and joyously with the earth.

Characteristics of an Earth Education Program

An Earth Education program:

○ Hooks and pulls the learners in with magical experiences that promise discovery and adventure.
○ Proceeds in an organized way to a definite outcome that the learners can identify beforehand, and rewards them when they reach it.
○ Emphasizes major ecological understandings (at least four must be included: energy flow, cycling, interrelationships, change).
○ Weaves the activities together with a clear, easily remembered organizing pattern.
○ Gets the description into the concrete through tasks that are both "hands-on" and "minds-on".
○ Uses what we know about good learning by building focussed, sequential, cumulative experiences that start where the learners are mentally and end with lots of reinforcement for their new understandings.
○ Avoids the labeling and quizzing approach in favor of the full participation that comes with more sharing and doing.
○ Focusses on building good feelings for the earth and its life as well as basic understandings of how it works.
○ Provides immediate application of its messages in the natural

world and later in the human community.
- o Pays attention to the details in every aspect of the learning situation.
- o Transfers the learning by completing the action back at school and home in specific lifestyle tasks designed for behavioural change.
- o Fits into the framework of earth education principles and guidelines.

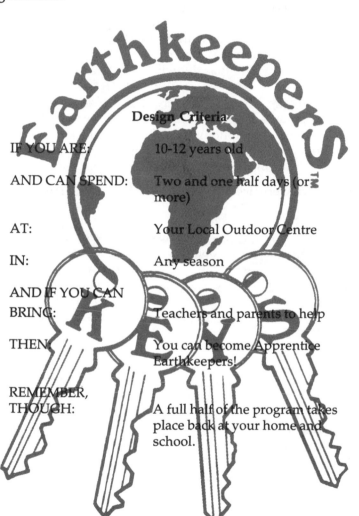

Earthkeepers

Design Criteria

IF YOU ARE:	10-12 years old
AND CAN SPEND:	Two and one half days (or more)
AT:	Your Local Outdoor Centre
IN:	Any season
AND IF YOU CAN BRING:	Teachers and parents to help
THEN:	You can become Apprentice Earthkeepers!
REMEMBER, THOUGH:	A full half of the program takes place back at your home and school.

THE EARTHKEEPERS PROGRAM

N ow that we've looked at the WHYS, WHATS and WAYS of Earth Education, let's get on with examining how the Earthkeepers program accomplishes these tasks. Earthkeepers actually begins at school on the day that a map of the Earthkeepers Training Center and a written invitation arrives in a classroom. The hobbit-like map apparently shows the location of some activities the students will be involved in, but the invitation is from a mysterious source known only as E.M. (pronounced em).

To set the stage for this initial contact experience the classroom teacher asked the students to spend some time the previous week looking into some of the environmental problems the earth faces and begin examining how the way people live contributes to those troubles. So E.M.'s invitation comes at just the right moment: the students know there are some serious environmental problems and an unexpected letter arrives asking them to become part of the solution.

For two weeks E.M.'s map hangs in a conspicuous position where the students can easily spot some of the other features of this unusual place: a swinging bridge, the old ruins, "wild things" hollow, and one whole area marked simply, "unexplored." You can imagine the slowly building excitement as the students dream about the adventures to come.

Naturally, curiosity about the identity of E.M. pops up daily as the students work on their preparations for the trip. (There are some key words to learn, special pouches to make, and a packing list and letter to take home to their parents.) However, to every query the teacher replies he doesn't know either and everyone will just have to wait until E.M. appears.

A Springboard Unit

The goal of the Earthkeepers program is to turn out youngsters who possess some basic ecological understandings and good feelings about the earth and its life, and will undertake not only to live more lightly themselves, but to share their insights and behaviours with others. Earthkeepers:

- understand how energy and materials tie all life together
- experience good feelings when they're in touch with nature
- undertake personal lifestyle changes in order to begin living more in harmony with the natural world
- help others increase their understanding of, feeling for, and harmony with the earth and its life

Obviously, in two and a half days we can only begin this task; much of it will have to be carried out back at school with the guidance and support of the classroom teacher.

Earthkeepers is for those teachers who genuinely want a learning adventure that will captivate and motivate their students, setting them off on a quest that must be completed later. It will not suffice for those looking for a brief, unrelated respite from the confines of the classroom or a primarily social, recreational outing. It's a fairly intense, highly stimulating educational experience that must continue for some time back at school.

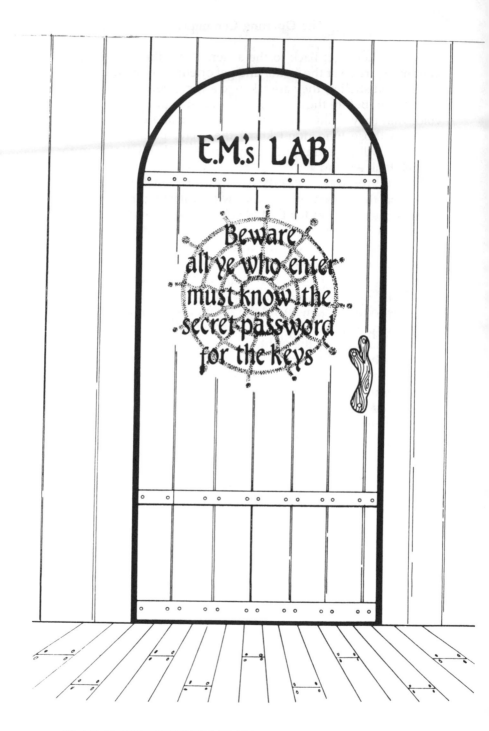

The Opening Ceremony

Okay. Let's get back to the action. After the Earthkeepers in training arrive at the center and get oriented to the necessities of food and shelter, they are taken to a very special room called, E.M.'s Lab. Before they enter, their trainer explains in a hushed voice that they really shouldn't be going inside because it's off limits to those who don't know the secret passwords, but if everyone will be extra quiet, they can all probably tiptoe in for a quick look around.

Inside, the room is fairly dark so each small group is led quietly to their seats by a helper with a flashlight. In front of them is the stage set for E.M.'s Lab, a magical nature nook lit by the glow of a brass kerosene lamp on E.M.'s desk just to the left of center stage. The three walls are lined with shelves and cupboards totally enclosing a slightly raised window to the right of the desk. (You can hear the sound of crickets drifting in from outside.) The shelves are jammed with assorted books, natural treasures, odd containers and the accumulated paraphernalia of a lifetime nature lover. There's a carved wooden rocking chair and an old trunk on the right.

The whole place appears like the owner just stepped out a moment ago. The chair rocks slowly back and forth in the flickering light of a nearby candle. Gradually, it comes to a halt, the sounds of the crickets fade away, and mysteriously, the shade above the window begins lowering of its own accord. Suddenly, soft music fills the room and a hidden projector beams a hazy image onto the white surface. At first, it's impossible to tell what it is, but as the image slowly comes into focus the viewers can make out that it represents the door of E.M.'s Lab: the opening picture in a very special slide show.

WELCOME

EARTHKEEPERS TRAINING CENTRE

Welcome to the Earthkeepers Training Centre. This is a special place where young human passengers are trained to be Earthkeepers. It is also a place where people can spend time enjoying the wonders of the natural world.

However, it is but a small part of a beautiful, fragile kind of spaceship – the Earth – which is powered by the energy of the sun.

The earth has its own interconnected life support systems to recycle its air, water, and soil.

All of the plants and animals that live on the earth are connected to these systems. They depend on them for the energy and materials they need to survive.

Unfortunately, many of the earth's human passengers don't understand how they are connected to these systems. Without realizing it, they are breaking their connections with the earth.

These broken connections are causing big problems for the earth and all the things that live on it.

And sadly, many people spend very little time in the natural world, enjoying its wonders and getting to know the other living things with whom we share the planet.

In many areas, the soil is being washed away by the rains and blown away by the winds.

In other places, the water has become harmful to the plants and animals that live there, including us.

Even the air is sometimes not fit to breathe.

And many people waste large amounts of energy.

You have come to the Earthkeepers Training Centre because the earth needs more Earthkeepers to help people renew and repair their broken connections.

An Earthkeeper is someone who understands how all living things on the earth are connected. An Earthkeeper has special feelings for the earth and wants to be in closer touch with it.

Earthkeepers make sure their personal connections with the earth are in good repair, and watch for and warn others about their broken connections before the damage is too great.

Earthkeepers also help others spend more time in the natural world, enjoying its wonders and marveling at its mysteries.

E.M. is the keeper of the keys – the keys necessary for unlocking the secrets of being an Earthkeeper.

It is E.M.'s job to help people renew their connections with the earth before it is too late.

E.M. knows a lot about the earth and the living things that share it. E.M. loves spending time in the natural world exploring new areas and getting to know our fellow passengers.

In front of you is E.M.'s lab. Here you can see some of E.M.'s favorite things... E.M.'s favorite rock from a special adventure... E.M.'s Diary on the desk... E.M.'s lantern for exploring the forest at night. E.M. comes here often to write in the diary about personal adventures and about the keys to becoming an Earthkeeper.

There are four keys you will have to earn to become an Earthkeeper like E.M.

The first key stands for knowledge. Earthkeepers understand how all livings things on the earth are connected.

The second key stands for experience. Earthkeepers realize that getting in touch with the earth is a good feeling.

The third key represents yourself. Earthkeepers believe that their actions on the earth make a difference.

The fourth key represents sharing. Earthkeepers know that helping others improve their relationship with the earth is an urgent task.

Here at the Earthkeepers Training Centre, you will receive your 'K' and 'E' keys after completing your training for knowledge and experience.

During this time you will be involved in special experiences and adventures that will also help you discover the secret meanings of E.M.

With your 'K' key, you will be able to open the 'K' box and learn the first secret meaning of E.M.

With your 'E' key, you will be able to open the 'E' box and learn E.M.'s second secret meaning.

To help you in your Earthkeepers training, you will also receive the Earthkeepers Training Manual and Earthkeepers Diary.

The Earthkeepers Training Manual introduces you to special adventures and experiences here at the Earthkeepers Training Centre. You will want to keep it with you at all times.

Like E.M.'s Diary, your Earthkeepers Diary is a place to write about your feelings for the earth during special times set aside for you to be alone in the natural world.

There are also some special people here to help you in your training. They are "Guardians" – the keepers of the secrets. You can recognize the Guardians because they will be wearing a medallion with a secret symbol on it – a symbol whose meaning you will discover as you go through your training. They will verify that you have completed a part of your training by signing your manual.

Guardians also let you know when you are doing something that will help you be a better Earthkeeper. They care about you and want to help you become an official Earthkeeper.

Trainers have already earned their four keys and want to share the secrets of becoming an Earthkeeper with you. They will guide you through the special adventures that await you here.

When you leave the Earthkeepers Training Centre, you will be an Apprentice Earthkeeper. You will have completed your training for Knowledge and Experience and will have received your 'K' and 'E' keys.

Back at home and at school, you will complete other tasks in your Training Manual to earn your last two keys.

After you complete the tasks for Yourself, a Guardian will give you a 'Y' key. This key will open the 'Y' box and reveal the third meaning of E.M.

After you complete the tasks for Sharing, a Guardian will give you an 'S' key. This key will open the 'S' box and reveal the fourth meaning of E.M.

Finally, after earning all four keys and opening all four boxes, you will become an official Earthkeeper – Level I.

You can then begin the important task of helping others renew their broken connections with the earth. Good luck with your training. And remember: E.M. will be with you.

Earthkeepers Schedule

RESIDENT

Day 1

10:30-noon	Arrival/Orientation
noon-1:00	Lunch
1:00-1:30	Opening Ceremony - E.M.'s Lab
1:30-2:45	"Munchline Monitors"/ "Great Spec-tackle"
2:45-4:00	"Great Spec-tackle"/ "Munchline Monitors"
4:00-4:45	Magic Spots
4:45-6:00	Class Time/Time Out
6:00-7:00	Supper
7:00-8:00	"K" Box/Mural
8:00-9:00	Evening Activities

Day 2

8:00-9:00	Breakfast
9:00-10:30	"Connection Inspection"/ "Time Capsules
10:30-noon	"Time Capsules"/ "Connection Inspection"
noon-1:00	Lunch
1:00-2:15	"E.M.'s Diary"/ "Earthwalk"
2:15-3:30	"Earthwalk"/ E.M.'s Diary"
3:30-4:00	Magic Spots
4:00-6:00	Class Time/Time Out
6:00-7:00	Supper
7:00-8:00	'E' Box/Mural
8:00-9:00	Earthkeepers Game Show

Day 3

6:30-7:30	Pack up/Clean up
7:30-8:30	Breakfast
8:30-9:45	"Seasons"
9:45-11:15	'Y' & 'S' Tasks/ Magic Spots/Pledging
11:15-11:30	Closing Ceremony - E.M.'s Lab

Earthkeepers Schedule

NONRESIDENT

Day 1

9:00-9:30	Opening Ceremony - E.M.'s Lab
9:45-11:00	"Munchline Monitors"/ "Great Spec-tackle"
11:00-11:30	Magic Spots
11:30-12:00	Lunch
12:00-1:15	"Great Spec-tackle"/ "Munchline Monitors"
1:30-2:30	"K" Box/Mural

Day 2

9:00-10:15	"Connection Inspection"/ "Time Capsules"
10:30-11:45	"Time Capsules"/ "Connection Inspection"
11:45-12:15	Lunch
12:15-1:45	E.M.'s Diary"/ Magic Spots (45 min.)
1:45-2:30	Magic Spots (45 min.)/ "E.M.'s Diary"

Day 3

9:00-10:00	"Earthwalk"
10:00-11:00	"E" Box/Mural
11:00-12:15	"Seasons"
12:15-12:45	Lunch
12:45-2:15	'Y' & 'S' Tasks/ Magic Spots/Pledging
2:15-2:30	Closing Ceremony - E.M.'s Lab

(Please note: When the timetable reads **"Munchline Monitors"/"Great Spec-tackle"** it means Group "A" does Munchline Monitors and Group "B" does Great Spec-tackle.)

"The Understanding Component"

Over the next two days the students will be involved in four concept-building activities called Conceptual Encounters. Focussing on the ecological concepts of energy flow, cycling, interrelationships and change, these activities are based upon the I-A-A learning model outlined in Sunship Earth:

I – Informing
(imparting knowledge about a natural principle or process)

A – Assimilating
(making the abstract concrete through actual physical engagement)

A – Applying
(reinforcing the intended outcome by transferring the understanding to the natural setting)

Or put more simply: the learners take something in, do something with it, then use it. The first section of the student's Training Manual deals with the informing and applying portions of each of these four primary earth education concepts.

For example, on the left hand page for energy flow the students read the key concept statement for the 'K' key, "All living things on the Earth are Connected," followed by a paragraph explaining the flow of sunlight energy. After reading this information (the Informing level of the model), the students participate in the activity, "Munch Line Monitors," to bring those words into the concrete (the Assimilating level). Next, they complete the task on the facing page which asks them to use what they have gained by finding an example of it in the surrounding area (the Applying level). When they have completed their examples, the students find a Guardian (a teacher or parent volunteer) to sign their manuals on that page documenting their work for the concept of energy flow.

At the end of the day, the students are ready to receive their 'K' Keys. The entire class assembles in the dining hall where they are broken up into small groups and given enlarged, black and white photocopies of one of the scenes from the slides in

the opening ceremony. Using coloured pencils they colour in these Earthkeepers' posters which will return with them to their classroom.

While the small groups of three or four students work on their posters, a trainer comes in and pulls one group out at a time to go with her to receive their 'K' Keys. Outside, she picks up a candle lantern and leads them quietly away from the lights and noise of the building. Then she circles them up to give each person the 'K' Key earned by his or her work so far.

"You've had quite a busy day here at the Earthkeepers Training Centre, haven't you," Karen begins softly. "I just want to check something out. Did you all get to visit Mama Nature's Munch Room and learn about the flow of sunlight energy through a munch line? Great. Let me see your training manuals to make sure you got the signatures you need for energy flow – open them up to page seven. Okay, everyone seems to understand the basic idea of energy flow. Next, turn to page nine so I can see if you got signed for materials cycling. Good, you followed air, water and soil specks and found that everything is made up of specks of material that travel in cycles and is used over and over again."

"You've done well. In fact, now that you have completed your first two knowledge tasks, you've earned your 'K' Key!"

Karen pulls a cloth pouch out of her pocket and reaches in to get a 'K' Key to hand to each person amid oohs and aahs of delight. "Now that you have earned your 'K' Key, it's time to open the 'K' Box and find out the first secret meaning of E.M."

The trainer explains that they are to proceed down a nearby path, using the candle lantern to light their way. When they come to a large boulder at the first bend, they will find the 'K' Box and each person in turn should use his or her key to open the box and discover the first secret meaning of E.M. (She adds that everyone should stay back a ways and let each person go forward alone to unlock the box and discover its secrets.)

On a card glued inside the lid of the box, lit by another candle lantern hung from the branch of a nearby tree, the students find the following passwords:

E.M. means
Energy and Materials

The box itself is filled with key rings, plus another card which says: "Congratulations. You have completed the first step in becoming an Earthkeeper. Take one key ring per person and put your 'K' Key on it. Be sure to lock the box when you are finished."

The trainer greets them when they return to the beginning of the path and asks if they know the first Secret of the Keys? Naturally, they reply enthusiastically that they do indeed, so the trainer asks them to turn to the page in their Training

Manuals that deals with the first secret and fill in the appropriate passwords as they repeat the questions and responses together:

Q. Why can you not do just one thing?

R. *Because all living things on the earth are connected.*

Q. What is the meaning of E.M. for knowledge?

R. *E.M. means **Energy and Materials***

Q. Can you prove it?

R. *I have the key to the box.*

Q. And what was written in the box?

R. *It says E.M. means **Energy and Materials** because that's what connects all living things on the earth.*

"Good job, now I can sign your manuals," Karen says. She takes Andy's manual and asks him, "Why can you not do just one thing, Andy?" *"Because all living things on the earth are connected,"* he replies. Karen signs his manual, then asks, "What is the meaning of E.M. for knowledge, Anne?" *"E.M. means energy and materials,"* Anne responds.

Karen continues until all the manuals are signed. "Remember, the meaning of E.M. for knowledge is a secret just for those who have earned their 'K' Key. Let's head back in now to continue working on our posters. Try to slip in quietly so no one notices. If they ask what you were doing, just tell them we were listening to the crickets or something. Don't show them your key yet!"

The trainer takes the group back in and pulls out another group of youngsters. She keeps taking these small groups until everyone has received a 'K' Key, each time emphasizing the importance of the questions and responses that deal with the passwords. From now on any Guardian or Trainer can ask a student at any time if he or she knows the first Secret of the Keys, and the student should be prepared to repeat the formal responses to those questions.

A New Kind of Filing System

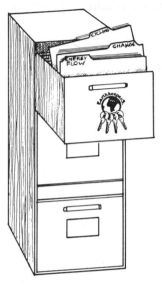

Think of ecological concepts as being like filing folders in the brain's filing system. They are mental categorizers.

Imagine for a moment that the human brain is a gigantic warehouse full of filing cabinets, each one crammed with great numbers of folders. In the past, nature educators (and sadly, most of our so-called environmental educators today) spent much of their time and energy trying to label and insert filing folders in those drawers for all of the thousands upon thousands of life's pieces. Frankly, this atomistic and reductionist approach has resulted for the average person in great numbers of mostly empty folders, topped with faded and tattered labels, jammed together in no apparent order.

We want to start over. We want to build and label fewer, more fluid folders that focus on the processes of life instead of its pieces. And we want to continue fattening up these folders back at home and school with lots of examples that relate to the participants' daily lives. In short, we want to reorganize the traditional filing system: we want our folders to represent function instead of form, flow instead of fossil.

To begin, we want to label one of those drawers in the system as "Planet Earth, Our Place in Space". Next we want to build some filing folders for that drawer dealing with the basic ecological concepts that govern life here, such as, energy flow and cycling. And on the tab of each of those folders we'll use the name of the appropriate concept along with a key statement that sums up the essence of these new understandings. In the Earthkeepers program we use the line, "All Living Things on the Earth are Connected" to get at the heart of what these concepts mean and tie them together in a whole.

Finally, the filing folder for each of our four key ecological concepts also comes with its own visual representation on the front:

energy flow	cycling	interrelationships	change

These four symbols add an important mental picture to the words for each concept and combine in the end to create a dynamic concept image for Earthkeepers itself. That symbol becomes E.M.'s shield throughout the program. Seen in the opening ceremony, in the training manual, and on the Guardians' mediallions, the meaning of the symbol is a mystery in  the early part of the program.[1] During each of the four concept activities the trainer wears a T-shirt with the appropriate logo on it (e.g., the energy flow logo during Munch Line Monitors). The logos are also incorporated into the example page for each concept in the training manual.

Due to the sequential nature of this image, these four symbols also serve as a visual "organizer" for the key concepts. You probably know from your personal experience that if you organize your own filing drawers, it's much easier to put things away and find them again later when you need them. So our symbols also serve as a way of organizing the filing folders in the students' drawers: from energy flow to cycling to interrelationships to change.

Together, the name of the concept, its key statement and visual representation, plus the visual "organizer" that pulls them together, help the students build, hold on to, and use these important understandings about life on earth.

---

[1]We believe this symbol will turn out to be one of the most powerful parts of the Earthkeepers program. We spent several years working on it, and we will probably use it in other programs we develop to help the participants visualize the four major concepts earth education must address.

The Basic Concepts

"Energy Flow"

Sunlight streams through space to bathe the surface of this planet each day. Green plants are the only living things which can directly capture this sunlight. Through the process of photosynthesis they package the sun's energy into molecules of sugar which build leaves, roots, seeds and other plant tissues.

As animals eat and digest plants, they open these packages of sunlight energy and use the energy to build their own tissues. And the energy travels even further when another animal (such as a hawk) eats the plant-eater (such as a rabbit). This path of energy flow, from the sun to plants to plant-eaters to animal-eaters, is called a food chain.

As energy flows along the food chain, much of it is used up and lost. Before they are eaten, plants use up much of their energy just to grow, and animals use up a great deal of sunlight energy as they move around. Because of this energy loss, there is less energy available further up the food chain, so in most food chains there are many plants, fewer plant-eaters, and even fewer animal-eaters.

"Cycling"

The basic building materials of life are hydrogen, carbon, oxygen, nitrogen, phosphorus and sulphur. There is a limited amount of these materials on earth, and they must be reused by all living things. They are constantly being taken up from and returned to the air, soil and waters of the earth.

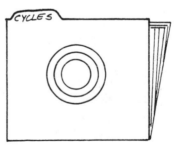

The soil is the great nourisher of plants, providing the nutrients which they need to grow. The soil would be useless if there was no way of getting these nutrients back after they had been taken out by the plants. But the soil is constantly being replenished, for there are millions of bacteria in each handful of soil that break down waste matter and dead animals and plants and return the nutrients which these things contain back to the soil. And so the cycling of soil reuses the building materials of life.

Water on earth is moved by the heat of the sun through a great water cycle. Water evaporates from the rivers, lakes and oceans of the world and rises into the sky where it condenses into clouds. From here the water falls back to the earth in the form of rain, snow, sleet or hail, only to flow once again into the rivers, lakes and oceans. Occasionally, the water takes a detour through a living thing. Evaporation and the filtering action of the soil are important purifiers in the cycling of water.

Parts of the air are also used over and over. With every breath animals of the earth exhale carbon dioxide. Plants use this carbon dioxide from the air when they make sugars in their leaves; and a by-product of this sugar-making process is oxygen, which the plants release into the air. Thus the cycling of air provides for the exchange of essential needs of life for both plants and animals.

"Interrelationships"

Living things are grouped together on the earth in specific communities because that is where they can best meet their needs of life. The actual place where something lives in a community, the place where it meets its needs of life, is called its home or habitat. A habitat may be as small as a beetle's tiny crevice in the bark of a tree or as large as an eagle's vast

hunting grounds; a good habitat takes up as much space as the plant or animal needs to find its food, shelter and water.

The role or job in the community performed by a plant or animal is called its niche. A squirrel basically occupies the niche of a tree-climbing seed-eater, while a bat's niche might be described as that of a nighttime flying insect-eater.

Everything in these communities is somehow connected to everything else. In meeting their needs, all plants and animals are constantly interacting with one another and with their surroundings. It would be impossible for any form of life to exist by itself.

Living things interact with one another in a variety of ways: often they are competing with each other for the same things (as when foxes compete with owls for mice), sometimes they are cooperating, although usually unintentionally (as when a squirrel "accidentally" plants trees as it stores nuts), but invariably they are depending upon one another for some part of their needs.

In reality, everything on earth is tied together in an enormous web of life. Like the web of a spider, when one strand is touched, all the other strands are affected.

"Change"

Everything on the earth is in the process of changing. In the lives and deaths of plants and animals, in the tides and winds, in the movement and flow of rock within the earth itself, we witness a dynamic, constantly changing planet in action.

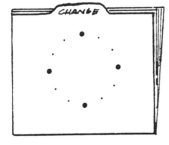

Many changes on earth occur so slowly that we cannot see them happening. The growth and movement of continents, glaciers, mountains and valleys take thousands of years. These and many other major earth changes require enormous amounts of time as their most important ingredient.

Certain changes in natural communities happen in a series of distinct stages. One such change is the succession of a new kind of plant which is able to live in the shade or soil built up by another kind of plant. A series of such stages can, over a long period of time, cover bare rock with a forest, and even though we could not witness the whole process in one lifetime, we can often see one or two of the stages of the change.

Every living thing has a built-in strategy which enables it to survive – a strategy to protect itself, get food and water, and reproduce. These strategies may take the form of special features – such as the webbed feet of an otter, the pinchers of a crab or the thorns of a shrub. In addition, the behaviour of an individual may also be part of this strategy. Trees lose their leaves in the winter, birds often fly south to warmer climates, and mice are usually active at night when they can be protected by darkness. Each living thing has a unique combination of features and behaviour patterns to solve its problems of living.

However, life is not static. Over time, life forms emerge with better fitting features and behaviour patterns and replace those which are less prepared. This process of adaptation is the cutting edge for the success of life on earth: those best fit survive in the end because they live to reproduce and pass along their improved strategies.

"The Feeling Component"

In Earthkeepers the feelings are just as important as the understandings. It's not enough to know; we want the students to care about what their knowledge tells them. We're convinced that it takes a combination of knowledge and experience to provide the supporting foundation for positive environmental action over the long term.

To accomplish this we focus on four components (Solitude, Discovery, Observation and Immersion) that we believe contribute to developing the emotion expressed in the key statement for the 'E' key: "Getting in Touch with the Earth is a Good Feeling."

Solitude

We want our learners to spend some time alone in touch with the elements of life: light, air, water, and soil. We want them to experience firsthand the richness and fascination of the flow of life in any natural setting. As Thoreau put it: "You learn that if you sit down in the woods and wait, something happens."

We also want our learners to have some time alone to reflect upon what's happening to them, i.e., to relate with the natural world, but also, to relate what they've been doing in our activities to their own lives. To meet this objective we set aside some time each day for the students to spend at their Magic Spots – quiet places in the natural world where they can sit and be alone in direct contact with the flow of life.

Observation

One of the many important things that we don't seem to make much room for in our present educational system is the skill of being a good observer. Frankly, lots of people miss much of what's going on around them.

Today, we live in the most energy intense societies in the history of the world and to survive we've unconsciously erected filters to protect us from the deluge of stimuli that wash over us each day. We simply don't see or hear or smell a lot of what's really happening in our lives.

When we take youngsters out of their urban-suburban

cultures and drop them down in a more natural setting, they're still wrapped in a veritable cocoon of these filters. In order to get them more in touch with life, we have to slow them down and help them peel away some of those filters with which they've encased themselves. Only then can they begin taking in any appreciable amount of what's going on out there. In another context, Aldous Huxley said you have to cleanse the doors of perception. We believe we have to peel away the filters so that our students can begin perceiving the intricate panoply of life that actually makes up their world.

In the Earthkeepers program we begin meeting this need by taking the participants on an Earthwalk, a light, refreshing nature walk that focusses on sharpening perceptions.

Discovery

It's not enough just to get the youngsters out there, you also have to arouse their curiosity about what's really going on. You have to help them discover that just a little momentary investment on their part can give them a tremendous return almost immediately.

Once they've found out that the communities of life represent an inexhaustible source of natural marvels and mysteries, we believe they'll want to continue their own poking, probing explorations whenever possible. The chilling exhilaration of making a personal discovery in the natural world is matched by few other emotions in life. We want our learners to have a taste of that experience and to hunger for more.

For the discovery component in this program, we use a vehicle that we call a Discovery Party, and the particular activity we designed for it this time draws upon both the enigma of E.M. and the participants' desire to explore some of the natural areas in their surroundings.

Immersion

Unfortunately, many youngsters come to an outdoor program today not only wrapped in filtering cocoons, but with some inherent barriers that prevent them from getting closer to nature. They've maintained their distance from the natural world for so long that they feel uncomfortable about such a simple thing as sitting on the ground. Getting wet and dirty are deeply engrained prohibitions that now serve as real barriers to building a personal sense of relationship with the earth and its life.

It's pretty hard to build a love affair with the earth if you don't have much contact with it. It would be like trying to establish a relationship with another person when you're in one building, your intended partner is in another one across the way, and the two of you never meet. By actually immersing ourselves in our surroundings, or by bombarding our senses with the stuff of our surroundings, we can begin overcoming some of these barriers in fairly dramatic ways.

In Earthkeepers, we do this by using an Immersing Experience, a barrier-breaking way of increasing the students' sensory contact with natural elements.

After the students have earned their 'E' keys through participating in these activities, they return once again to the dining hall on the second evening to work on a class project while awaiting a trainer. This time small groups work on filling in the outlines on a large, collage-style mural representing their experiences at the Earthkeepers Training Centre, but instead of going back to the forest, after they receive their 'E' keys, they are taken to E.M.'s Lab itself.

"Take this lantern," Martin explains, "and go into E.M.'s Lab. Open up the 'E' box one at a time and read the instructions inside. Be sure to lock the box again, then come back out here when you're finished. I'll be waiting for you."

The trainer hands the candle lantern to one of the group and everyone enters E.M.'s Lab – a little nervously, but terribly excited. Inside, the room is dark except for a small kerosene lamp lighting up the 'E' box on E.M.'s desk. The sound of crickets can be heard once again in the background and the whole atmosphere creates a hushed, expectant tone.

Huddled around the lantern, the group waits while Carrie goes up to the desk first. She unlocks the box with her 'E' Key and opens it to reveal the second secret meaning of E.M. – "E.M. means My Experience." Another card attached to the back wall of the box reads:

"You have completed the second step in becoming an Earthkeeper. Take one Apprentice Earthkeeper Card. Lock the box when you are finished."

Outside, Martin asks, "What did you find out?" "*E.M. means My Experience*," Carrie responds. "*That's what we learned about today,*" Chad adds. "Great," says Martin. "You've learned the second secret meaning of E.M. There are two other meanings you will learn when you earn your other keys. Right now though, get out your manuals and open them to page 20. Those are the questions and responses you should know now that you have an 'E' Key. Fill in the two blanks on that page with the passwords you discovered in the box, and then we'll read through them for practice."

When they are finished, Martin asks each question again and the group softly reads the response out loud together:

Q: Why should you increase your contact with the earth?

R: *Because getting in touch with the earth is a good feeling.*

Q: What is the meaning of E.M. for experience?

R: *E.M. means **My Experience**.*

Q: Can you prove it?

R: *I have the key to the box.*

Q: And what was written in the box?

R: *It says E.M. means **My Experience** because that's how I can increase my contact with the earth.*

Afterwards Martin signs their manuals and reminds them that they now know two passwords: E.M. means Energy and Materials because that's what connects all living things and My Experience because that's how they must increase their own contact with the earth.

"The Processing Component"

The third and most important of the Earth Education "Whats" is Processing. In Earthkeepers the understandings and feelings the students gain in the activities required for earning their first two keys serve as motivators for earning the last two.

One of the most innovative aspects of the Earthkeepers program is that the learning doesn't end after a three day visit to an outdoor center. Fully half of the program must be completed when the students return. For Apprentice Earthkeepers the all-important steps of applying their new knowledge and experience to their own lives and sharing it with others must take place back in their classrooms and homes. Consequently, they earn their 'Y' and 'S' keys through a series of additional tasks carried out after they leave the Earthkeepers Training Centre (See Appendix).

The Closing Ceremony

On the final morning the students are given two flyers that outline their options for earning their remaining keys. Each flyer contains a series of tasks that they will choose from in order to complete their work. After looking over the information in the flyers, the students head off to spend some last moments at their Magic Spots, and while there decide upon which of the tasks they will pledge to complete for earning their 'Y' and 'S' keys. They note their choices on a copy of the Pledge Page from their Training Manuals and return with them to E.M.'s Lab.

Inside, the Lab is just as it was before except that now the 'K' and 'E' Boxes are open revealing the secret passwords written on the inside of their lids. Once again, the rocking chair gradually comes to a halt, the sound of the crickets fades away and the shade above the window slowly descends to become a screen for another slide show.

Welcome back to E.M.'s lab, Apprentice Earthkeepers. You have completed the first part of your training.

Two of the secret meanings of E.M. have been revealed to you.

When you used your 'K' key to open the first box, you discovered that E.M. means Energy and Materials.

During your training for this knowledge, you learned how sunlight energy flows through a food chain when you became munch line monitors.

You saw how all materials are recycled as you traced the paths of famous specks.

You then became connector inspectors and realized that energy and materials tie all living things together.

You even found an old time capsule and learned how everything changes over time because of the effects of energy and materials.

You also received your 'E' key and opened that box to find that the second secret meaning of E.M. is My Experience.

You experienced the natural world in many ways during your training, including spending time alone at your own Magic Spot thinking about what it means to be an Earthkeeper and getting to know your special place.

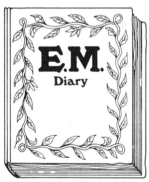

You followed E.M.'s diary, not only to find one of E.M.'s favorite places and treasures, but to discover your own.

You got in touch with the earth in some unusual ways when you went on an Earthwalk.

And you experienced a season using senses other than your sight.

Although you've received your first two keys, your training is not complete. You are Apprentice Earthkeepers and must complete the tasks you've chosen in order to receive your last two keys and open the 'Y' and 'S' boxes.

As you complete your tasks for lessening impact and deepening feelings you will learn that your own actions on the earth make a big difference. Afterwards, you will receive your 'Y' key from your teacher and can open the 'Y' box to learn another secret meaning for E.M.

When you finish your sharing tasks, you will get an 'S' key from your teacher and open the 'S' box to learn the fourth meaning of E.M.

You will then have completed your apprenticeship and will be a full-fledged Earthkeeper – Level I.

Remember, though, as an Earthkeeper, you will need to continue working on your own environmental habits and sharing your experience with others.

Perhaps someday you will go through further training to become an Earthkeeper – Level II.

Next, you would get more training before becoming an Earthkeeper – Level III.

You might even return to the Earthkeepers Training Centre to earn your Level IV and Level V designation.

And maybe one day you will become what we are all trying to become – a Master Earthkeeper.

After the slide show, the Director of Training steps forward to E.M.'s desk:

"There's a note here on the desk addressed to the Apprentice Earthkeepers. Let's see what it says:"

Congratulations. You did it! I'm proud that you've done so well in becoming Apprentice Earthkeepers. I hope you realize how important it is that you complete your tasks and become full-fledged Earthkeepers. Without more Earthkeepers, I'm afraid the earth is in big trouble. Go back home now and earn your last two keys – discover the secrets of the 'Y' and 'S' boxes – and become genuine Earthkeepers. Do it for the earth!

I'll be with you,

E.M.

"After you've completed your 'Y' and 'S' tasks you will get those keys from your Guardian and open those boxes in your classroom."

With that, the Director of Training takes his 'Y' key and sneaks a peek into the 'Y' box, so that no one else can see. He does the same with the 'S' box, then addresses the group again.

"E.M. left a note for us, let's leave a message for E.M. As you depart, come by the desk and leave the Pledge Page from your manual here, so E.M. will know about your commitment to earning your last keys and discovering their secrets."

The Apprentice Earthkeepers file past the desk, leaving their pledges, and head outside to begin the next part of their training – living as Earthkeepers.

The Follow-Through

Back at school the Apprentice Earthkeepers continue with their training. Encouraged and supported by their Guardians they begin working on the tasks they pledged to undertake in order to lessen their own impact on the earth, for the 'Y' Key represents Yourself: "Your actions on the earth make a difference." When their new behaviours have been faithfully performed for at least one month, they bring in their 'Y' task flyer (signed by a parent) and their Guardian presents them with a 'Y' key (Appendix "A").

The 'Y' Box can be set up in a special corner of the classroom, or even better, in a special place in the school (like an exhibit case devoted to Earthkeepers). Inside, the students will find the third secret of E.M. (My Earth) and receive their Earthkeepers button. Afterwards a Guardian will once again check out their new understanding about these additional passwords before signing their Training Manuals.

Q: Why should you examine how you use energy and materials?

R: *Because your actions on the earth make a difference.*

Q: What is the meaning of E.M. for yourself?

R: *E.M. means* **My Earth**

Q: Can you prove it?

R: *I have the key to the box.*

Q: And what was written in the box?

R: *It says E.M. means **My Earth** because
     my actions here make a difference.*

The apprentices are now ready and eager to push for their final key, the 'S' key. 'S' stands for Sharing since "Helping others improve their relationship with the earth is an urgent task." To earn it the participants must share both their knowledge and their experience with someone else.

The tasks outlined in the 'S' key flyer require that each student has to become a leader, guiding someone else through four of the same activities he or she has experienced (Appendix "B").

For example, that person may be a friend, a brother or sister, or even a parent or other relative. Whoever it is, the student must actually set up the activities and guide the person through them, not just talk about them. (Special prop sheets for this purpose are contained in the packet of Duplication Masters for the program.)

When a student brings in a signed 'S' task flyer to the Guardian, and explains what was done, it is cause for a special celebration. First, the student uses the 'S' key to open the last box and discover the fourth secret meaning of E.M. This time when the student looks down into the box, a mirror, placed on an angle in the bottom, reflects his or her own image and the meaning of E.M. becomes clear: E.M. IS ME. A card on the back of the box reads:

> "Congratulations. You have completed the fourth and
> final step in becoming an Earthkeeper. You are now an
> Earthkeeper - Level I. Take one of the yellow beads and
> attach it to the cord on your key ring. Don't forget to
> lock the box when you are finished."

Waiting nearby, the Guardian recites the final (by now almost ceremonial) questions:

Q: Why should you share your Earth-
     keepers experience with others?

R: *Because helping others improve their
     relationship with the earth is an urgent
     task.*

Q: What is the meaning of E.M. for sharing?

R: *E.M. means **Me***

Q: Can you prove it?

R: *I have the key to the box.*

Q: And what was written in the box?

R: *It says E.M. means **Me** because it's up to me to help others improve their relationship with the earth.*

Q: And who is the real keeper of the keys?

R: ***I am** the keeper of the keys.*

Q: And who are you?

R: *I am **E.M.***

Finally, the student's name is inscribed on the roster of Level I Earthkeepers that is kept next to the 'Y' and 'S' boxes, page 35 from the student's training manual is sent in to the institute and an official Earthkeepers certificate is sent in return. Then an announcement is made to the entire school that from now on the earth has another helper – a person who will demonstrate in his or her own behaviours the attitude of a true Earthkeeper.

EartlikeeperS™

has successfully completed
Earthkeepers™ Training
and is an Earthkeeper™
in good standing

Level III
Earthkeeper

Level IV
Earthkeeper

Level I
Earthkeeper

Level II
Earthkeeper

Level V
Earthkeeper

_____
Guardian

_____
Director of Training

_____   _____
Training Center   Date

The Institute for Earth Education

THE KEYS TO BECOMING A TRAINER

"Hookers and Organizers"

A "hooker" is the initial experience that sets the kids up to want to participate in a learning activity. We always said in our Acclimatization work that we wanted to pull the kids in, not push them. So the hooker is the motivator; it pulls the learners in and motivates them to want to carry out the learning tasks we've established. A hooker turns a boring worksheet into an exciting task. A hooker turns an authoritarian teacher into a learning helper. A hooker turns a listless kid into an energetic participant. Hookers can be as elementary as a special invitation and map delivered to the classroom before an adventure, or as elaborate as our "Welcome Aboard" ceremony in Sunship Earth.

The "organizer" is a device that helps the participants hold onto the points learned. It aids them in keeping track of what's happening and increases their chances of putting the learnings to some use. An organizer can be as simple as using the word HOMES to remember the names of the Great Lakes (Huron, Ontario, Michigan, Erie, and Superior), or as complicated as EC-DC-IC-A, the formula we use in Sunship Earth for explaining the ecological story of life on our planet (E = Energy Flow, C = Cycles, D = Diversity, C = Community, I = Interrelationships, C = Change, A = Adaptation).

The overall hooker of the Earthkeepers program is the invitation to become an official Earthkeeper; an invitation delivered in the magical setting of a lab that belongs to a mysterious, unseen character known only as E.M. This idea provides the context within which everything else takes place.

The organizer that helps the learners keep track of what they are learning in the program is the word, KEYS. In E.M.'s Lab, they find out through their training tasks in four important areas (Knowledge, Experience, Yourself, and Sharing), that they will not only discover the secret meaning of E.M., but also become Earthkeepers themselves. Thus, in Earthkeepers we have a double organizer: the secret meaning of E.M. deals with the conceptual understandings and their internalization, and E.M.'s K-E-Y-S tie the various facets of the program together.

E.M.

The enigmatic, shadowy E.M. dominates the Earthkeepers program. E.M. is everyone's dream of the wizard of the woods, a munificent recluse who lives alone but loves to share the marvels and mysteries of nature in unusual and secretive ways.

E.M. is sexless and colourless, but probably a bit older, hopefully, a bit wiser. E.M. provides a very powerful image, a hooker that will captivate and motivate learners, but it's an image that must be handled with great care. Since no one ever sees E.M., we must be very careful to provide just enough of an outline that the learners can fill in the details provided by their own imagination, yet not go too far. We have to walk a very fine line between reality and fantasy.

Remember: A hooker is used to pull the learners into the educational experience, not the leader's influence. And we don't want E.M. to dominate the activities to the detriment of their messages, nor become so bold, so fully-fleshed that the revelation at the end about E.M.'s identity will prove disappointing. Actually, the less said about E.M. the better. For in the end, E.M. turns out to be an ephemeral hero, but don't despair, for like the ephemerals of the forest, E.M. returns again in Earthkeepers – Level II.

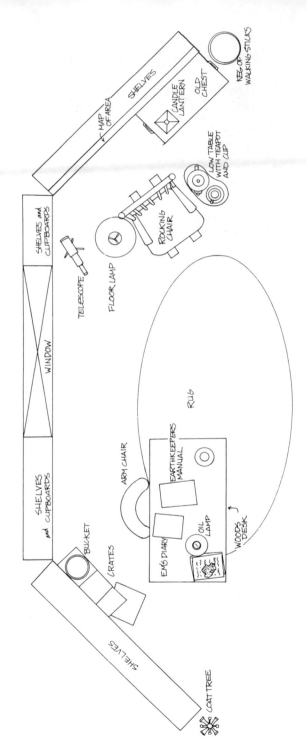

E.M.'s Lab

Picture the interior of a kindly old nature lover's special workroom. Part study, part retreat, the whole place is suffused with the feeling of its owner.

This is nothing like the usual sterile lab, nor is it filled with preserved and stuffed creatures unfortunate enough to have been collected for "scientific" study. It's a bit cluttered, inviting exploration. It's the kind of place you would really like to poke around in for a while; a place filled with the detritus of a lifetime of roaming the land, of living closely with the natural world.

Formed by three walls, one of which contains an old-fashioned sash window, the room includes a simple wooden desk, a carved wooden rocking chair, an ancient trunk (with an old candle lantern sitting on it), a keg of walking sticks and a coat tree. Next to the rocking chair there's a floor lamp made from the trunk of a tree and a low, cloth-covered table holding a teapot and a cup. In one corner there's a pile of wooden crates and metal buckets with a pond net leaning against them.

Cupboards make up the bottom third of the walls, while the upper area is covered entirely with shelves (completely enclosing the window with its old, pull-down white shade). A framed map of the area hangs over the shelves on one side.

The only light comes from a brass kerosene lamp on the desk and a couple of candle holders clipped onto the edges of the shelves.

Those shelves are filled with natural treasures picked up on countless expeditions: skulls and assorted bones, gnarled pieces of wood and chunks of fossils, a jar of seed pods, a kaleidoscope, a framed picture of a fox, a couple of shells, maybe a hornets nest or the head of a sunflower.

Numerous unusual containers, wedged in among lots and lots of nature books (heavier on the stories than the identifications), include small chests, odd-shaped tins and one or two sturdy baskets with solid handles. You can't quite tell what some of these things are, yet in their very lack of clarity they invite participation.

Scattered around the room you'll find much to catch the eye: perhaps an old microscope, a pair of snowshoes, a homemade geologic model, a simple telescope mounted on a wooden tripod; certainly a cloth bag or two, a carved wooden bird, a piece of an antler, a pair of binoculars. Once you settle in and your eyes adjust to the dim light you may notice four wooden boxes stuck here and there and labeled with one of the letters, K-E-Y-S, or hear the entrancing sound of crickets drifting into the room from beneath the open window.

On the desk there's a colourful rock for a paperweight, some pencils and a couple of feathers in an old clay pot, a large magnifying lens with an antler handle, and conspicuously: a Training Manual and the owner's personal Diary.

Locks and Keys

The locks and keys required for the program are available through The Institute for Earth Education. The keys are brass and have the word "Earthkeepers" on one side of the keyhead and the appropriate letter ('K', 'E', 'Y' or 'S') on the other side. The keys are cut to fit only the corresponding lock, and the locks (laminated steel padlocks) are keyed alike so that every 'K' key will open every 'K' lock but not 'E', 'Y' or 'S' locks, and so on.

One of the most incredible hits in the Earthkeepers program is the reaction of the participants when they receive their first key and see that it's a real key that opens a real lock – and they get to keep it! While the idea of E.M. and the opening ceremony in E.M.'s Lab are enough to get them to buy into the program, that first key is what "locks" them in for good.

General Notes – "Hookers and Organizers"

1. E.M.'s Lab is not the home of the "mad scientist", but the refuge of a friendly, yet shy nature lover. A little extra effort attending to the details here will make a difference in the "hooking" power of this crucial phase of the program.

2. Since E.M.'s Lab is essentially a stage set, you may want to recruit someone involved in theatre work to help you put it together. Some centre's will also need to make the entire set highly mobile. In this case, any "streamlining" required must be offset by paying even more attention to the details in the workmanship and the quality of the materials used.

3. The Earthkeepers Keys can be used for other things both at the centre and back at school. Once a key has been earned it should "unlock" other discoveries and rewards for the participants.

4. Paint your locks black so they will look older and blend in better with the boxes.

 **"Roles and Ceremonies"**

Trainers – The Leaders of the Experiences

Trainers are the leaders in charge of helping young people become Earthkeepers. They are responsible for setting up the Earthkeepers program, providing pre-trip materials to the classes, leading activities at the Training Centre, and assisting the teachers with the completion of the program back in the classroom. Each centre has a Director of Training who is the primary contact person between the centre and The Institute for Earth Education. The director is responsible for training the other trainers and the guardians, and for maintaining contact with the participating schools. In a small centre, this person is also often involved in leading the activities.

Trainers must have a thorough understanding of both the Earthkeepers program and our leadership guidelines. Trainers for Level I need to be at least Level I Earthkeepers themselves; Trainers for Level II need to be at least Level II Earthkeepers, and so on. Here is a summary of how trainers become Earthkeepers and advance in their own training.

Level   Training Required

I   **Studying** (read entire set of Earthkeepers program materials)

         Training (participate in at least one of the following)

         ○ Attend a day-long Earthkeepers program introduction at an Earth Education conference or staff meeting
         ○ Serve as a Guardian for an Earthkeepers – Level I program at an accredited Earthkeepers Training Centre.
         ○ Attend a thorough staff training session at an Earthkeepers Training Centre.

         Processing (complete the following personal tasks)

         ○ Incorporate one new way to use less energy or materials into your daily routines.
         ○ Participate in a new natural experience.

II   **Studying** (read Level II program materials)

Training (participate in at least one of the following)

○ Attend an Earthkeepers – Level II program introduction at an Earth Education conference or staff meeting.

○ Serve as a Guardian for an Earthkeepers – Level II program at an accredited Earthkeepers Training Centre.

○ Attend a thorough staff training session at an Earthkeepers Training Centre.

Processing (complete the following personal tasks)

○ Analyze your lifestyle in terms of your energy and materials use and prepare a plan for making improvements.

○ Go on a solo experience in the natural world.

Training requirements for the other levels follow the same framework of these three main components: studying the materials, training for that level, and processing the insights through personal tasks. Individuals who complete their training may write to the Institute for an application to obtain an official Earthkeepers certificate.

It is important for all those who wear Earthkeepers keys to have earned them. It makes a big difference to the students to find out that their Trainers earned their keys and beads by taking part in training and working on their own lifestyle improvements and personal relationships with the natural world.

Remember that one of our most important guidelines is to model positive environmental behaviours. Trainers should be constantly aware of all the little details that reinforce what the program is trying to convey – turning off the lights when leaving a room, being gentle with living things, eating lower on the food chain, not using "throw-away" containers – actually being an Earthkeeper!

Guardians – the Keepers of the Secrets

Guardians are teachers, parents, volunteers or other adults who help with the Earthkeepers training. During the program they:

○ Assist the Trainer with the activities.
○ Recognize and reward the participants who are doing a good job in their training by giving them special badges to wear.
○ Sign the manuals at the completion of each task.
○ Reinforce the understandings and appropriate behaviours.

sharing

In addition to the above responsibilities, a teacher's role as a Guardian includes:

○ Preparing the class before the visit to the Training Centre.
○ Supervising the participants throughout the program.
○ Helping the participants with the 'Y' and 'S' tasks and giving the 'Y' and 'S' keys and the Earthkeepers certificates.

Guardians should have a thorough introduction to the program, preferably at the Training Centre, before their visit. Guardians helping with the program for the first time earn their keys along with the participants; at the end of each activity, the Guardians get their training manual signed by the Trainer before they help sign the participants manuals. Of course, Guardians need to work on tasks to receive their own 'Y' and 'S' keys as well. Guardians may earn their keys and beads in the same way Trainers do; unlike the Trainers though, the Guardians do not need to have their keys before the participants receive theirs.

Guardians are recognized by the medallion they wear. It is a wood disc with our concept logo etched or painted on it. The participants discover the meaning of this symbol as they complete their knowledge tasks.

E.M.'s Boxes

The K-E-Y-S boxes play a very special role in the Earthkeepers program. Their appearance should reflect their importance; make sure they look both old and earthy.

Construct the boxes of wood – about 12 inches across the front, 8 inches wide and 10 inches deep (30 cm X 20 cm X 25 cm). Using rough, distressed wood in aged, natural tones – perhaps with black corner plates – will convey the necessary feeling.

Each box should have a hinged lid with a hasp on the front for the lock. One of the four letters should also be painted (or etched and painted) on the side of each and the appropriate explanation and instruction cards glued inside.

Four boxes (one for each letter) are needed for E.M.'s Lab, four boxes (one of each letter) go to each classroom, two 'E' boxes are needed for "Seasons," and nine 'K' boxes are needed for "Time Capsules." You will also need a 'K' and an 'E' box for each class to use in the Key ceremonies. The boxes in the classrooms should stay there for the remainder of the school year and can be returned to the Earthkeepers Training Centre then (or when the next class returns the following year) to be refilled with 'Y' and 'S' awards.

General Notes – "Roles and Ceremonies"

1. If you would like to prepare your staff for setting up the Earthkeepers program, contact us at the Institute. We may be able to arrange for a trainer to come to your centre or for your staff to visit an accredited Earthkeepers program at another centre.

2. Teachers who bring their students to an Earthkeepers program need to know beforehand that they must play a fairly active role both at the centre and back at school. They will certainly not be able to stand back as disinterested spectators. Earthkeepers cannot succeed in its mission without the ongoing involvement and support of the classroom teachers.

3. The role of the Guardian is to make sure that the secrets are understood by the "initiated." However, Guardians should be cautioned not to present themselves as obstacles to be overcome but as supporters who must substantiate.

4. In a non-resident setting, the box ceremonies are done during the day and so take a little more set up to create the hushed tone and serious mood that is so easy to achieve at night. In this case, it may help to assign a role to each person in the group – e.g., one leads the way to find the box, another opens it, another reads the top card to everyone, another reads the bottom card, another hands out the rewards inside and another locks the box and leads the group back. This approach may also be useful in night ceremonies with groups that need more structure and control.

5. In the 'S' box a mirror is placed at an angle on the bottom so that when the students open the box and look inside they will see their own reflections (after they read E.M. means ME). Glazing compound will hold the mirror securely in place.

6. The Earthkeepers posters that the students work on during the box ceremonies are available from The Institute for Earth Education.

 **"Tools and Tasks"**

Manuals and Diaries

At the Earthkeepers Training Centre each student receives a Training Manual and a Diary, and carries them at all times in small, waterproof pouches.

The manual helps guide learners through their experience at the center. "Look," says Rich, after passing out the manuals, "It's a note from E.M."

"Welcome to the Earthkeepers Training Centre. I'm glad that you are here and are ready to begin your training. The earth needs your help!"

The manual spells out specifically what an Earthkeeper must do and describes the different levels leading to becoming a Master Earthkeeper. (A Master Earthkeeper has a model relationship with the earth and its life that all Earthkeepers are striving to achieve.)

"All living things on the earth are connected," reads a student from the manual. Prior to embarking on the first concept-building experience the group forms a circle and the leader asks the students to take turns reading, out loud, three short paragraphs about energy flow. This informing stage of the activity prepares the learners for what they are about to learn. It tells them "where they are going." To help keep everyone on track, the manual is organized in four sections. The first is the 'K' (knowledge) section including energy flow, cycling, interrelationships and change. Next comes the 'E' (experience) section with solitude, discovery, observation, and immersion, and finally, the 'Y' (yourself) section for lessening impact and deepening feelings and the 'S' (sharing) section for sharing knowledge and experience. Each activity page has a box at the bottom where the leaders sign their names signifying the successful completion of that particular experience.

After each major section, "The Secret of the KEYS" documents that the student knows the passwords for that part of the program. For example, the following questions and responses appear at the end of the 'E' section:

Q: Why should you increase your contact with the earth?

R: *Because getting in touch with the earth is a good feeling.*

Q: What is the meaning of E.M. for experience?

R: *E.M. means _____*

Q: Can you prove it?

R: *I have the key to the box.*

Q: And what was written in the box?

R: *It says E.M. means _____ because that's how I can increase my contact with the earth.*

This format is also designed as an additional assurance that we are getting mental as well as physical engagement ("mind's on" as well as "hand's on" involvement). And the built-in success of being able to answer the challenge offers an additional measure of confidence ("*I can do it!*" "*I am knowledgeable and capable.*" "*I have earned my key.*")

Later, other Trainers and Guardians will ask the students again if they know the secret of one of the keys, and each time they must reply with the appropriate response to the questions for that key. This repetition reinforces the major objectives of the program and gives the students a way of continually adding to their understandings without forgetting what they've already gained.

Throughout the Training Manual notes from E.M. keep the students tuned in to what's happening, and on the inside of the back cover a final note from E.M. congratulates them for completing the first part of their Earthkeepers training: "You now know and care about the systems of life and realize your impact upon them. You also know that you are not finished being an Earthkeeper but are just beginning, just as you understand that this is not 'goodbye' but 'hello'!"

Another important tool in the Earthkeepers program is the Earthkeepers Diary. Each student receives a diary and is encouraged at different times throughout the program to record things that relate to his or her relationship with the earth. Many students use some of their Magic Spot time to think about and write about the natural world. The first pages of the diary contain a message from E.M.

It's so quiet here in my magic spot that I can hear the breeze rustling one small leaf on the plant next to me. I enjoy my magic spot; I can think here. Sometimes I write my thoughts down in my diary.

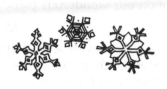

I always write in my diary at least once each season; all Earthkeepers should. Even if I'm not in my magic spot, I still write down the neat natural places I've visited and the new plant and animal passengers I've met.

I also use my diary to keep track of how I'm doing as an Earth-keeper. It helps me look at how I'm gaining new knowledge, ex-periencing nature, lessening my impact on the earth, and shar-

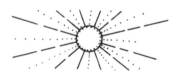

ing all of this with my family and friends. After all, an Earthkeeper never stops trying to be a better friend of the earth.

I thought you might enjoy a diary like mine. Begin using it at the Earthkeepers Training Centre and keep adding to it at least once each season. I think that you'll find that it helps you keep in touch with something that's very, very important – your relationship with the earth.

After this note, the diary goes on to ask the students to get to know their Magic Spot and then to write down some things about it. Other pages begin with the first few words of a sentence intended to help the students begin writing about their experiences at the centre. Another section helps them look for signs of each of the four seasons. E.M. wants them to write in their diaries at least once each season, not only at the centre but particularly when they return home. Their diary can become their special, personal record of their journey to becoming an Earthkeeper and living more in harmony with the systems of life on our wonderous planet.

Mealtimes

Meals provide a great opportunity to reinforce understandings and behaviours and to relate the concepts that are being learned to our daily lives. Here are some things to do:

o Recognize those who have earned special reward badges (given out by the Guardians) by having them stand for a round of applause.
o Use "Waste Watchers" (see Sunship Earth) to cut back on food (packaged sunlight energy) waste.
o Present the "Mystery Muncher" (see "Mystery Passenger" in Sunship Earth).
o Serve wholesome, nonprocessed foods that are low on the food chain.
o Eliminate "throw-away" containers or serving materials (discourage their use if the participants bring their own lunches).
o Set up a compost pile outdoors or a worm compost bin indoors for any organic waste. (Use the compost to grow luffas for cleaning sponges!)
o Use a munch tray to analyze what kinds of munchers are being eaten at a meal.
o Display disguise-removing menus for the meals (see Sunship Earth).

Apprenticeships

The role of the teacher as a Guardian is especially important in the completion of the program back in the classroom. The participants have earned their 'K' and 'E' keys and are now Apprentice Earthkeepers. To earn their last two keys they must practice being a true Earthkeeper. While the responsibility of completing the tasks belongs to each individual student, the teacher can do a great deal to help.

The 'Y' and 'S' task flyers are designed to explain the tasks to parents as well as ask for their help in verifying that the tasks have been completed. The activity descriptions in the flyer for the "Sharing knowledge" tasks explain how to set up and lead each activity. The accompanying prop preparation sheets, with instructions on making props for the activities, can be given to each individual so everyone can make his or her own set of props to use for the two activities to be shared, or small groups can work together on the props for an activity and then anyone who has chosen to share that activity can use them.

Setting up a corner of the classroom (or an exhibit case in the hallway) with the four boxes, plus the mural, pictures and poems from the visit to the Training Centre, key statements, rosters listing those who have earned their 'Y' and 'S' keys, and the like can provide a good way of keeping up interest. Of course, the teachers should always wear their Guardian medallion when giving out a key and can make the experience special by adding touches and details that let the students know they think this is something important (e.g., hosting an evening key ceremony similar to that experienced at the Training Centre).

When the 'Y' and 'S' manual pages have been sent in to the Training Centre and the certificates received, parents can be invited to an all-school assembly to recognize those who have earned all their keys and are now full-fledged Earthkeepers.

Most importantly, the teachers need to show a personal interest in the program by wearing the keys, working on their tasks, and modeling being an Earthkeeper themselves.

Earthkeepers Bulletin

One of the most commonly expressed frustrations felt by the staff of many outdoor centres is the lack of ongoing contact with groups that have visited their site. In addition to being designed so the program does not end when the visit to the centre is over, Earthkeepers also has a way to keep in contact both with classes and with individuals – the Earthkeepers Bulletin.

Using a masthead provided by the Institute, the staff of the Training Centre sends periodic Bulletins to classes that have participated in the Earthkeepers program. Stories, poems and drawings that Earthkeepers have submitted can be included; hidden "connections" can be revealed; special weekend experiences for Earthkeepers can be highlighted; and advanced training opportunities can be advertised. The Bulletin is a good tool for maintaining contact between the Training Centre and the schools as well as helping keep the program alive back in the classroom.

Advanced Training

Completing Earthkeepers – Level I doesn't mean the end of involvement. Many Earthkeepers Training Centres offer special weekend experiences for Earthkeepers; these often include discovering new natural areas, providing Magic Spot time, and looking at new ways of reducing energy and materials use. Training Centres may also offer advanced levels of Earthkeepers Training.

Earthkeepers – Level II brings E.M. back to life as the Master Earthkeeper. A powerful introduction in E.M.'s Lab begins three days of acquiring new knowledge by setting out on three Earth Secrets Concept Paths (each with three concept-building activities from Sunship Earth). New Magic Spots are found and new experiences (Immersing Experiences and Discovery Parties from Sunship Earth) help the participants get in closer touch with the earth. A closer look at individual ways of using energy and materials also sets the stage for new tasks to be completed at home to become an Earthkeeper – Level II and earn the second coloured bead. Schools that participate in both the Earthkeepers and the Sunship Earth programs can use the entire five day Sunship Earth program as Level II training.

Earthkeepers – Level II is open only to those who have completed all of their 'Y' and 'S' tasks to become an Earthkeeper – Level I. It has been offered successfully as a summer program in both residential and nonresidential settings.

Earthkeepers – Level III takes place a year after Level II training and, of course, is open only to those who have completed their Level II tasks and earned their second bead. It involves three days on-site in a residential setting, so Earthkeepers trained at a nonresidential Training Centre need to go to another Training Centre for Level III. Such a trip can provide a great opportunity though for experiencing new natural places, meeting Earthkeepers from other areas and feeling a part of something much larger than just a local group.

Level III is based on our SUNSHIP III program and is designed for junior high age students (13-15 year olds). The entire program, from activities to lodging to meals, focusses on exposing the often hidden ways we use energy and materials. It successfully channels the very traits which so often discourage centres from attempting an outdoor program with this age group into a powerful experience with great impact.

Level IV training uses our Earth Journeys ("Group Journeys" in <u>Acclimatizing</u>) to help the participants get to know various wild places. Level V training, when completed, will use our projected Earthways program. Designed for 16-19 year olds, Earthways focusses on a small group of young adults who help each other on their personal quests seeking the end of the rainbow. Finally, Earthkeepers – Level VI are Master Earthkeepers, but the secrets to becoming one are only revealed to Level V Earthkeepers.

Centres interested in offering additional Earthkeepers training (Levels II-V) should contact the Institute's program coordinator.

General Notes – "Tools and Tasks"

1. Each participant needs a weather-resistant pouch for the training manual, diary, pencil and other materials used during the three days at the Training Centre. The pouch should be a bit larger than the training manual and have a cord sewn in that is long enough to go around the head and one arm. It should be made of heavy material (the water-

repellant nylon used in backpacks works well – check with canvas supply companies for seconds) and have a top flap to keep out the rain. You may be able to enlist the help of a sewing class to make them. A set of well-made pouches kept at the Training Centre can be used by participants during their three days on-site and will last for years.

An alternative is to have each participant make a pouch at school before the visit to the Training Centre. While this adds a nice personal touch, helps build anticipation and enables the participants to keep the pouch to use back at home and school, the trade-off is that they are often not made of high quality or water-repellant materials and don't hold up to weather and heavy use; care must be taken with this option to provide clear instructions on size, materials and construction details.

2. The best way to encourage students to write in their diaries is for you to write in yours, and then to share with them individually what each of you recorded. (Just be sure to keep such sharing non-threatening and non-evaluative.)

3. Over the years we've noticed that there's a fairly strong tendency for some leaders to take a minor part of a program (say, a mealtime skit or evening campfire) and turn it into the major production of the entire experience. In the end the students may go away remembering more about one of these supplemental performances than the messages they were intended to support. We've often said that we don't believe we stifle creativity in our work so much as channel it, but you must still be very careful that a creative surge does not end up dominating an unexpected portion of your program.

4. Since the Earthkeepers Apprenticeships take place back at home and school, we would hope that the goal of every school participating in the program would be to see that every student earns his or her 'Y' and 'S' key through a genuine and lasting change in environmental behaviour. Just as we want every student to learn how to read and write, we should want every student to learn how to live more lightly on the earth. The future of our planet depends upon it.

THE EARTHKEEPERS ACTIVITIES

'K' - Conceptual Encounters

"Adventures in Learning Ecological Principles"

Conceptual Encounters are highly participatory and stimulating ecological concept-building learning experiences. We call them encounters because meeting up with them (both in their content and methods) represents an unexpected adventure for the participants. Designed for a classroom group of 20-30 students, they originated in <u>Sunship Earth</u>, where they were called the "Interpretive Encounters."

While the "Concept Paths" in the Sunship Earth program focus on building several concepts through a series of short activity stations set up along a trail, the Conceptual (Interpretive) Encounters focus on building just one concept over a longer period of time. Most encounters take from one to two hours to complete.

Conceptual Encounters are designed to meet the following criteria:

- focus upon developing a deeper understanding of one ecological concept
- emphasize peer-to-peer interactions in the learning process
- utilize a problem-solving storyline
- involve ongoing roles for the participants
- require the leader to set up and direct the overall activity

In addition to the above criteria, the Conceptual Encounters in the Earthkeepers program were also designed to be used in a variety of settings and situations. In fact, much of the piloting was carried out in cold, snowy weather.

General Notes – Conceptual Encounters

1. Be sure to read the introductory material and study the general notes that accompany each activity in the separate "Conceptual Encounters" binder containing the detailed narrative descriptions (available from The Institute for Earth Education).

"Munch Line Monitors" Overview
(Energy Flow)

Try to imagine achieving any understanding of the environment without first grasping energy flow. It's literally the key to understanding life on earth. In Earthkeepers the concept of energy flow comes to life at Mama Nature's Munch Room where the learners become "Munch Line Monitors." The objective of this activity is to enable the students to see for themselves how energy flows from the sun to green plants and on to animals, creating a food chain or "munch line." By using the analogy of a lunchroom, a familiar organizing metaphor, the learners move easily through successive steps in the activity.

They begin by reading key conceptual information on energy flow in the Earthkeepers Training Manual, statements which are reinforced by a visual representation of the sun set up to demonstrate sunlight energy flowing from the sun to plant to animal to carnivorous animal.

Once outside, the learners are invited to become Munch Line Monitors, but in order to qualify, they must go through some special training. First, the students get triangular badges to wear identifying them as monitor trainees. Each "point" on the badge represents one step of the outdoor portion of this activity and is checked off or punched at the appropriate time of completion. Armed with grocery store counters, the "monitors trainees" begin by finding first-hand evidence of "munching" in the area and record, by quantity, all of their evidence. When the totals from all the teams are tabulated and displayed to the group, the kids are amazed to see just how much "munching" is going on all around them. Next, every team gets a compartmentalized "munch tray" (an actual lunch tray painted with an arrow to represent the flow of sunlight energy from compartment to compartment), and the trainer instructs them to fill their trays with evidence of the

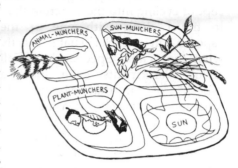

munchers. There are sun-munchers (plants), plant-munchers (herbivorous animals), and animal-munchers (carnivorous animals). Of course, the learners must figure out for themselves which compartment would be appropriate for each "find" they make in the natural world. Soon they are called back to tabulate their results again. This time the number of sun-munchers is recorded by separate hatch marks on the bottom of a large tablet; just above them go the hatch marks representing the plant-munchers and so on. The kids watch intently as a food pyramid, made up of many sun-munchers, fewer plant-munchers, and even fewer animal-munchers is formed before their eyes. Finally, the teams each get a "munch bag" (an actual lunch bag filled with examples of different parts of a food chain). They find a quiet spot to fill their munch trays with the items in their bags, and when they are ready, they trade with another team to see if they can figure out the munch line that group represented.

After their badges are complete, they return to their manuals and draw and label their own example of a food chain whose parts they can see nearby. Finally, the trainer reinforces each person's work by signing the manual in the designated spot.

The students are now trained and ready to "monitor" other food chains. The trainer even gives them some examples from everyday life to broaden their understanding of what they've just learned. It's clear, all living things on the earth are connected, through the flow of sunlight energy.

"Great Spec-tackle" Overview
(Cycling)

What better way to get the concept of cycling into the concrete than to travel along with one of the "specks" in a cycle! That's exactly what the "Great Spec-tackle" is all about. Participants even meet a "speck" of air that Marco Polo breathed, a "speck" of water that Cleopatra drank and a "speck" from a prehistoric dinosaur. At Speck Trail Junction, the journeys of representative specks (molecules enlarged enough to be visible) from each of the great biogeochemical cycles – air, water and soil – are actually laid out so their courses can be followed.

Before going outside, the group assembles and reads the key conceptual information on cycling from the manual. Afterwards, the trainer brings out three bags and asks if someone would hold her stock of "air specks", "water specks", and "soil specks", then explains that everything is made up of some combination of these three types of specks – specks that are used over and over again. As she points out that familiar parts of the natural world like a plant, a rock and even a person are made up of these specks, the trainer asks for varying proportions of specks from the bags and constructs model examples to illustrate her comments. Next, lengths of yarn are used to demonstrate how yet other specks are cycled through all living things.

Once outside, a note from "Solid Sam" is found along the trail. When everyone arrives, the trainer reads it, and they hear about the adventures of one particular soil speck named Solid Sam.

They are really in for a treat though, when further down the trail they stumble across Speck Trail Junction. At that spot, the trails of many different specks converge at one main point and then head off in all different directions. There are soil specks like Earthy Earl and Howie Humus. There are water specks like Liquid Larry and Sally Splash and air specks like Soaring Sal and Light Lucie. These

specks each have a story to tell about what they've been a part of in the past and, after teams are formed, the trainees go out and follow one speck at a time through each important cycle. They can't help but notice that the cycles are connected because each speck trail crosses a point in common with the other two cycles. After each team has followed one speck from each cycle and thought of their own example of where the speck could be headed next, the group gathers again. They listen to the trainer read a postcard from a speck who has encountered problems in her travels. Pollutants, as they accompany each speck, can build up and be impossible to get rid of in the cycle. Finally, the participants are made more aware of these problems through some everyday examples.

And in the end, they get to pinch that speck of a dinosaur. Each other!

"Connection Inspection" Overview
(Interrelationships)

Since they're invisible, the connections between living things are pretty tough to see, but in "Connection Inspection," these relationships become easy to see.

The activity begins in front of a large web of dark blue, light blue, brown, and yellow cord, in shape similar to the symbol on the guardians' medallions. The trainer uses the web to explain how everything is connected by the use of energy and materials.

Next, the participants locate connections in the woods around them. Using a special "Connection Scope" (a plastic tube with one end bisected by a strand of wire), they connect a tree to the soil (a soil connection), a bird to a tree (an air connection), and the sun to the grass (an energy connection). All of these interrelationships provide one or both things involved with something they need to survive.

Afterwards it's time to connect themselves. Each student becomes a plant or animal from the area, and using their own dark blue, light blue, brown, and yellow cords, they connect themselves to their sources of water, air, soil, and energy by using a 'K' lock and their own 'K' key to "lock into" the things they need. A frog might attach his water strand to a post labeled lake and his energy strand to a person playing a mosquito, since he gets his energy from eating that mosquito. The mosquito, meanwhile, is hooking her air strand up to a bush, the source of her air, just as the bush is connecting his energy strand to a post labeled sun. When everyone is finished, they are all connected into an incredible "Web of Life".

It's clear that this complicated web of interrelationships supports all life, but what will happen to the web if someone does just one thing, like draining the lake? Will very many other things be affected?

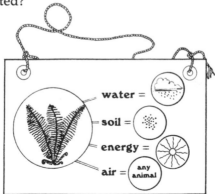

To find out, the trainer unlocks the 'K' lock at the lake post to break the connections of all those who need the lake for water. Every living thing that finds one of its connections broken drops all of its connections in turn. Everything that finds one of its connections affected by that action drops its connections, and so on. Soon, the whole web is broken apart. Since all living things on the earth are connected, we cannot do just one thing.

"Time Capsules" Overview
(Change)

Over time, the flow of energy and the cycling of materials through living and non-living things changes those things and the other things around them. Materials such as air and water, moving through great cycles powered by the energy of the sun, change the landscape. Living things are constantly changing so they can get and use their energy and materials in better ways. Everything is changing all of the time. It is this constant change that keeps life going.

E.M. has left the group a curious map. In addition to the creek and hills they can see around them, notations also mention a shallow sea and a volcano. What kind of map is this?

It's a map that will help the students trace the history of the area by leading them to nine buried time capsules, capsules filled with artifacts from different periods in the history of this place. With the 'K' key they earned the day before, they can open the capsules, match up the things inside with a mural showing that time period, and then arrange the artifacts on the "Time Shelves". These shelves are labeled 3,500,000,000 years B.N. (Before Now), 500,000,000 years B.N. and so on up to the present day.

The artifacts represent the stages and changes this land and its life have undergone. For example, three and a half billion years ago, volcanoes dominated a lifeless landscape, and the items in the capsule from 3,500,000,000 years B.N. – from a model volcano to samples of cooled molten rock – illustrate this history. 100,000,000 years ago huge dinosaurs roamed the earth. Just 20,000 years ago, a great sheet of ice covered the land to the north, and primitive people had begun to use stone tools, like those found in the Time Capsule for that period, to hunt the woolly mammoth.

Throughout this historical record, the path of a single soil speck is also traced. This dot turns up on a fossil fish, on the tooth of a dinosaur, on the forehead of the trainer today. Following the path of that speck, the trainer guides the group through the incredible changes that have taken place in the past and wonders how the things we're doing now will affect the future. Are we sometimes stopping natural change from happening? Are we changing other things too quickly or drastically? Could we go the way of the dinosaurs?

'K' – Earthkeepers Game Show
"Reinforcing the Main Points"

The live studio audience buzzes excitedly in anticipation of the Earthkeepers Game Show which is about to begin. (Pre-game excitement has been building throughout the day after a series of special announcements were made in the dining hall at lunch and supper.)

Now that the crowd is seated, they are able to see the large Earthkeepers Game Show Board in front of them. Attractive letters spell out the name of the game show at the top of the panel, while a series of brightly colored signs announce the question categories immediately below. Sets of cardboard pouches matching each category color form a series of columns stretching down the panel and a question card sticks out from the top of each pouch.

The "guest celebrities" are introduced with lots of hype and fanfare as the host greets the crowd:

"Welcome Earthkeepers trainees, Guardians, ladies and gentlemen and viewers at home, to the Earthkeepers Game Show! Have we got an exciting show in store for you tonight!

(Applause Sign)

Join us as our Earthkeepers in training match wits and test their skills by answering questions from a range of topics. But first, let's meet tonight's guests..."

The Show

"Okay, I think we're ready to begin the show. First of all, there will be two teams, Team E and Team M.

"The objective of the game is for each team to spell out the word Earthkeepers and at the same time get as many points as it can.

"To receive a letter, each team must correctly answer a question. If answered correctly the team receives that letter and the points for that question.

"For each question (letter), there is a point value – 1 for an easier question and 2 for a harder question. Each team may choose which type of question it wants.

"A representative from each team will come down on stage and choose: 1) a letter, and 2) the point value.

"Let's recap how it works:

o Rep will choose letter and point value.
o Host will ask the question.
o The rep will re-join the team to agree on the answer. After arriving at an answer, the rep will come back on stage.
o The host will ask the question once more.
o The rep will then respond.
o Correct Answers – get points and letter
o Incorrect Answers – question is passed on to opposing team and they have a chance to answer the question. Opposing team though only gets the letter or the point value (not both).
o REMEMBER: Try to spell the word Earthkeepers and get as many points as you can"

General Notes – "Earthkeepers Game Show"

1. The staff should maintain a fun atmosphere in which participation is encouraged and competition doesn't become the main emphasis. The students are contestants as well as the studio audience (waving at imaginary T.V. cameras, applauding during breaks, etc.). However, you must guard against letting the magic overwhelm the messages. Don't let your staff get so carried away with their roles that the students remember their antics and forget the points they were reinforcing.

2. The group should be split into two teams at the beginning of the game (avoid making up teams too early as competition tends to overshadow learning).

3. Use the "celebrities" to remove the questions from the pouches, to turn the EARTHKEEPERS letters around as they are earned, to bang a gong for correct answers, etc.

4. One way of assuring a tie is to keep the number of question cards in each pouch hidden from view so the host can "run out" of questions when both teams are tied. The "Bonus" questions can also be used to award extra points to a team and keep them in the game.

Prop List – "Earthkeepers Game Show"

1. Game Show Board – for displaying questions
   - ○ a large cardboard panel, attractively designed to catch attention
   - ○ a large title at the top: **Earthkeepers** GAME SHOW
   - ○ "category headings" located beneath the title, i.e., Munchline Monitors, Great Spec-tackle, Guardian's Choice, Trainer's Bonus
   - ○ a series of cardboard pouches (cardholders) in columns corresponding to the categories (see diagram)

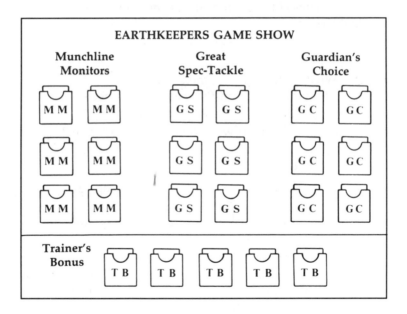

2. Sets of Questions
   - ○ typed onto index cards and laminated
   - ○ categorized as easy or hard
   - ○ answer typed at bottom of each card
3. Two sets of individual letters spelling the word "EARTHKEEPERS" (should be in bold print and laminated on separate cards).
4. Display board/panel for Earthkeepers letters.

5.   Costume ideas for celebrities:
- ○   host - tacky, loud jacket and tie (possibly a hat)
- ○   judges - fake nose and glasses, loud jacket
- ○   hostess - evening gown, forearm length evening gloves, flowery hat

Sample Questions – "Earthkeepers Game Show"

1.   Q: What do Guardians guard?
     A: The secrets of the keys

2.   Q: From what sources do people get their energy?
     A: Plants and animals that are eaten (or the sun through them).

3.   Q: What is at the beginning of every munchline on earth?
     A: The sun

4.   Q: What is another name for a speck?
     A: A molecule

5.   Q: What is the key statement for the 'K'?
     A: All living things on the earth are connected

6.   Q: What is the key statement for the 'E'?
     A: Getting in touch with the earth is a good feeling

7.   Q: What is the secret meaning of E.M. for the 'E' box?
     A: My Experience

8.   Q: Arrange this munch line in order: frog, grass, grass hopper, sun, raccoon
     A: Sun, grass, grasshopper, frog, raccoon

9.   Q: Who is E.M.?
     A: An Earthkeeper, or the Keeper of the Keys

10. Q: Clouds drop rain, the air takes it back again. It forms into clouds, the clouds drop rain again. What is it?
     A: The water cycle

11. Q: What four things come together to form the web of life?
     A: Air, soil, water, energy

12. Q: I've been in a flower, a bee, and a tree. Can you figure out me?
     A: A speck

13. Q: When do you become an apprentice Earthkeeper?
     A: When you have achieved the 'K' and 'E' keys

14. Q: Which is used over and over again, energy or

materials?

A: Materials

15. Q: What do you call a place where you can enjoy some quiet time to get in touch with life?

A: A Magic Spot

16. Q: What are the three kinds of building materials everything is made of?

A: Soil, water, air

17. Q: Give an example of a sun-muncher, a plant-muncher, and an animal-muncher.

A: Any plant, any plant-eater, any animal-eater

18. Q: When do you become an Earthkeeper?

A: When you have achieved the 'K', 'E', 'Y', and 'S' keys.

19. Q: What is the secret meaning of E.M. for Knowledge?

A: Energy and Materials

20. Q: I've floated down a river, I've sailed in a cloud, I've even washed your dishes. I'm not too proud. What am I?

A: A water speck

21. Q: What did the skull and crossbones stand for on the speck trail?

A: Pollution specks, poison specks

22. Q: How can a munchline get messed up? (Name one way)

A: Anyway a food chain can be interfered with

23. Q: Are there more sun-munchers or animal-munchers on earth?

A: Sun-munchers

'E' – Earthwalks
"Light, Refreshing Touches of Nature"

In the Earthkeepers program we use an unusual kind of nature walk to help the participants begin experiencing the natural world in a different way.

An Earthwalk is a special technique for introducing some of the marvels and mysteries of nature. It is a light, refreshing approach for getting closer to the earth and its life.

An Earthwalk is made up of a series of special activities, usually from four to six, put together in a smooth, flowing way. The length of the entire experience is from about forty-five minutes to one hour and fifteen minutes.

On an Earthwalk the participants get to know some of nature's subtleties: the world underfoot, the simple wonders often overlooked, the micro-marvels seldom seen. However, the leader is the guide here, not the focal point. The focus is on the natural world. Although the leader may introduce the activity and see it through, the emphasis is on the doing and sharing by the participants.

Just as important as the activities selected is the flowing way in which the leader ties those activities together. The leader doesn't just say, "Come on over here". Instead, the method for getting from one activity to the next is built into each activity itself. Thus, the participants are enticed along from activity to activity as the walk progresses, and by the end, it will have seemed like one continuous experience. A good Earthwalk is synergistic; it is more than the sum of its parts.

Setting up a Walk

Here are some tips on preparing an Earthwalk. Take a quick tour of the area where the walk will take place. Identify the activities you wish to use. There are over 75 of them available, but remember 4-6 are plenty for one walk.

When you want to cover a bit of ground between two activities, choose an activity that will get you from one place to the other in the process. (We call them "ambulators.") Now arrange your activities so that the end of one leads into the beginning of another. Try to eliminate the choppy, stop-and-go, "follow-me, gather-round" approach of the typical nature walk.

You may need to create a bit of glue to go between the activities (perhaps a pinch of fantasy or a special role).

The following sources contain Earthwalk activities (along with more detailed instructions on setting one up):

<u>Acclimatizing</u>
(called a "Quiet Walk")

<u>Sunship Earth</u>
(called "Touch the Earth")

<u>Earthwalks</u>
(called "Earth Magic" and "Snow Walk")

General Notes – Earthwalks

1. An Earthwalk should start where the leader meets the learners and end at the place where the leader leaves them. Remember: There must be some type of participatory role for each person in each activity. There are no "observers."

2. Ordinarily, an Earthwalk should not depend upon prior set up. The trainer should carry everything needed.

3. Spend a lot of time getting your props ready and practicing how you will use them. An Earthwalk leader should come across as a special kind of nature wizard.

4. Most important: an Earthwalk is an adventure, not a natural history recitation. And please don't play "Twenty Questions" with your participants. We want them to feel caught up in the experience, not threatened by what they're supposed to be learning.

5. Avoid "processing" the walk. Let it stand on its own. You can build in a sharing activity, but for the most part, you should be doing things, not talking about doing things.

6. Let's face it: Most nature walks are rather boring. That's probably why most people don't go on them. So infuse your walk with some excitement about the wonders of the earth. You're the all-important catalyst for success.

'E' – Magic Spots
"Special Places to be Alone in Touch with Life"

A young boy sits alone, leaning comfortably against a tree trunk. He is by himself, but knows that his friends and leaders are not far away. There is no sound of human voices, no noise but the murmurings of the branches in the wind, some birds singing, a stream meandering on its way, a single leaf scuttling along the ground. He comes to this special spot he has chosen in the forest to pause and reflect, to ponder and dream. He looks up to see the pattern of the branches of "his" tree against the sky, leans back to feel its bark against his skin, reaches out to touch the soil at its roots. This is his Magic Spot.

A Magic Spot is a very special place to be alone and bask in the richness of nature. On the first day of Earthkeepers the students individually select a particular Magic Spot and throughout their stay at the Earthkeepers Training Centre, they visit their spots to spend some time alone with the natural-world. Each group leader guides his or her group to a desig-nated, separate area and before they select their spots, the spec-ial idea of Magic Spots is explained. They are cautioned to be very careful about selecting one small spot from so many pos-sibilities. "Your spot should be out of sight and hearing from other chosen spots, if possible," suggests the leader. "It should be a place where you can sit comfortably, with a good tree or stump or rock to lean against." The leader recommends that they look in their Diaries for some possible things to do while spending time at their Magic Spots. "You don't have to do just those things," she adds. "Those will help you become familiar with your spot, but basically, your Magic Spot time is a time to sit quietly alone and just tune in to the flow of life. That's the overriding goal here."

For one of their Magic Spots times, the group leader suggests applying some sensing techniques practiced during their Earthwalk – listening, smelling, touching – perhaps searching for patterns of light and shadow, etc. At other times, the Diary inputs suggest exercises which will help the youngsters listen to different sounds, scrutinize small things, and focus on the many scenes of their special places.

An unusual technique for one of these times is called "Seton-watching." The leader explains, "Today at your Magic Spot, try some Seton-Watching. Ernest Thompson Seton was an artist and writer in the early 1900's, who based his paintings and stories about nature on the countless hours he spent observing the natural world. This activity is named after him because, just as he did, you'll get to know the plants and animals near your spot." The leader then tells a story about a time when she was Seton-Watching and a squirrel came up and sat right next to her foot: "I was so quiet and still that the squirrel didn't even pay attention to me. When you sit very still like that, the natural world just sort of settles down around you like you're not even there. You may not see animals every time, but you are more likely to. Besides, you're also more likely to feel lots of other things."

"If you'd like to Seton-Watch, the best way is to find a tree or stump to lean up against where you can sit very still for a long time. Sit down and make sure you are completely comfortable. Sort of run through your muscles mentally to see if there is any pressure," she explains while demonstrating. "Then, when you're fully comfortable, take a couple of deep breaths and relax. As you breathe, settle into a state of motionlessness. Don't move at all, but don't strain. Just relax and let the natural world sweep over and engulf you."

After explaining Seton-Watching, she takes the group to their Magic Spots. They try it, and some of them report later seeing birds, animals, insects, even falling leaves that they hadn't noticed before. They saw many things that go on there when they usually weren't present. Most importantly, they began to feel the flow of life around them.

At the end of each Magic Spot time, the leader blows on a horn or conch shell to signal the students that she will soon come down the trail to have them join her. In the meantime, they have spent a few moments in a quiet place, where each is alone with his or her personal thoughts. Magic Spots provide a good environment for the youngsters to make the connection between problems of the entire planet and this one special place they have begun to value. The more they get to know this place, the more they will respect and remember one small piece of the natural systems of our preeminent home: Earth.

General Notes – Magic Spots

1. The success of this activity depends upon the location of the Magic Spots. The trainers should lead their groups to a specific area and then drop them off one at a time to look for their spots within a clearly defined space ("between the big tree and the rocks"). With a large group the trainer can wander silently through an area with the students lined up behind her. For each person, in turn, the trainer points to a good spot. If the youngster likes it, he or she sits down. If the student spots a better one nearby and points to it instead, the trainer either nods in agreement or shakes her head no and points out another. Of course, none of the spots should be in view of one another.

2. Before the initial Magic Spot time, the trainers should set the stage very carefully:

   ○ Talk in a hushed voice to set the tone.
   ○ Make a pact with the group not to infringe on the rights of fellow group members (including talking, moving around, hooting, whistling, etc.).
   ○ Explain the signal for the end of Magic Spot time.
   ○ Circle the group up and ceremoniously pull down the veil of silence, all together, signaling absolute silence. (Then lift the veil together when the group gathers up at the end.)

3. Before the first couple of visits, the trainer should present

to the group some suggestions for things they might think about or do while at their spots.

4. If the woods or fields are wet, ask the kids to bring their raincoats to sit on, or have "sit-upons" (squares of ensolite pads or carpet samples work well) for them to use.

'E' – Discovery Parties
"Explorations Emphasizing A Sense of Wonder and Place"

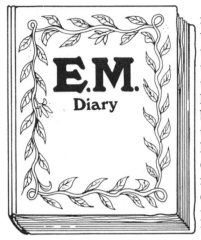

It's quite a sight: twenty or more kids on hands and knees, with magnifying lenses pressed to their eyes. Looking closely at their new "Miniature World," they find inch-high jungles, delicate ice crystals, sturdy pebble boulders, intriguing holes, and the squiggly residents of a dead log. With the help of a quaint old map and a diary kept by the mysterious E.M., they've been exploring an area not many people get to see. Their task is to retrace a previous adventure of E.M.'s (and have one of their own along the way). With each student taking a turn leading the group, they've not only found this "Miniature World," they've also found their own "Listening Posts," discovered a secret hiding place, and crossed a creek on fallen trees. Before they return to their starting point, they will have found a special treasure (one that can fit in the palm of their hand), and then left it behind for future explorers of this wild area.

A Discovery Party is a vehicle designed to build a sense of wonder and place. Taking advantage of the students' innate sense of wonder and desire to explore, it encourages individual "finds" and personal exploration, with just enough structure to hold the group together. It is a "party" because it is a gathering with a bit of a festive atmosphere about it, as well as a group working together to perform a task. For the leaders, a Discovery Party offers a chance to respond with wonder and knowledge to the discoveries the students make. The leaders can share morsels of natural history information of their own with the kids who have found something that intrigued them. Or, they can encourage further exploration and discovery by suggesting more interaction with the item (e.g., I wonder what it smells like?). For leaders and students alike, a Discovery Party is a free-wheeling exploration of the natural world.

"E.M.'s Diary"

"E.M. likes to explore and poke around and discover neat things and special places," Martin says. "Sometimes E.M. writes about adventures in a diary like the one you've been using. Do you remember the diary on the desk in E.M.'s Lab? It describes an adventure E.M. had exploring an area around here that hardly anyone ever goes into; we thought it would be neat to go there and use E.M.'s diary to help us explore it and relive E.M.'s adventures. Would you like to go along?"

Of course, the adventure appeals to the participants, even more so when Martin reveals a map. "E.M. drew a map of the area to go along with the diary. I've made copies for you to use, too." Martin gives each group of two or three a map, and they spend a couple of minutes looking it over. Then they are off to the wild area, a place where they've never been before.

When they reach the area where the map begins, Martin circles the group up and has them look at their copies of the map as he reads the first entry from the diary:

> Today, I decided to spend some time exploring an area I'd never been to before. It's fun to check out places where not too many people go. So I headed down a faint trail through the forest. When I crossed a small dead log on the trail, just before it went down a little hill, I started through the trees to the right.

"There's the faint trail leading into the forest!", someone exclaims.

"Then let's head down it," Martin suggests. "Remember to keep a look out for the small dead log on the trail, before the trail goes down a little hill. Stop when you find the spot where you think we should head off to the right."

Off they go! Martin reminds them to walk softly and look carefully, but a couple of kids charge off down the trail ahead, going right past the spot they were looking for. The others call them back, and when they are all together, Martin reviews the first entry and asks if everyone agrees that this is the right spot. They do, so he reads the second entry:

> I stopped to look at a hole a small animal ran into right after I crossed the big log, and I think that's when I left my walking stick leaning against a tree somewhere. I didn't notice till later that it was missing, but I don't

recall having it after that. Maybe I'll find it when I go back there someday.

The entire group searches for the walking stick. Several possibilities are found, but they are quickly discarded when someone calls out, *"Hey, now this is a walking stick!"* She holds up a gnarled old staff for all to see. *"It even has E.M. carved into it."*

"Great!" Martin says. "Maybe we'd better leave it here though for E.M. to find on a future visit." After they lean it back against the tree, Martin circles the group back up and reads the third entry:

> I continued on through the forest, keeping a little ways away from the edge of the hill. Suddenly, I came upon a sort of open area filled with all kinds of small, interesting things to look at. I called it my "Miniature World". I got out a "third eye" to help me look more closely at things, got down low, and began to explore.

The group soon comes to an area like the one E.M. described. Martin hands out "third eyes" (hand magnifiers) for everyone to use, and they spend a few minutes poking around in this Miniature World. Martin then pulls the group back together and reads the next entry:

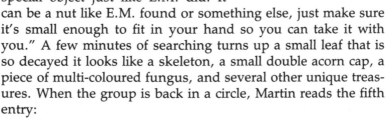

> I found a really neat little nut that stood out from the others for some reason. I'm not sure if it was its size or color or shape or even where it was that made it so different, but I picked it up and looked at it very carefully – feeling it, smelling it – and finally decided to hang on to it for a while. So I took my new friend along with me.

"Why don't we each find one special object just like E.M. did. It can be a nut like E.M. found or something else, just make sure it's small enough to fit in your hand so you can take it with you." A few minutes of searching turns up a small leaf that is so decayed it looks like a skeleton, a small double acorn cap, a piece of multi-coloured fungus, and several other unique treasures. When the group is back in a circle, Martin reads the fifth entry:

> I decided to go down the hill to the creek, but the hill

was a bit too steep right there. I went further up along the top of the hill and I came to a log lying across what looked like an old trail heading down the hill. I went down there instead.

Martin asks anyone who finds the spot to wait at the top, so they can all make sure it's the right way. Some groups study their maps carefully while others head off like bloodhounds on a hot scent. A couple of possible places are spotted, but in the end they all agree on one that fits the description perfectly. Martin has them go down the hillside in a single line, side-stepping, because it is still rather steep. At the bottom the group pulls together so Martin can read the sixth entry:

I was amazed. It was like I'd gone to a whole new place. The forest floor was much more open here, and the trees were so much bigger! I found one really neat big old tree to check out more closely.

"Hey, I bet that's it over there," someone calls out. "Or maybe that one."

"Before we go to the tree we think it might be," Martin cautions, "let's find out what else E.M. says about it." He reads the next entry:

What an incredible living thing that tree was. I bet it's older than anything else around there. It felt so sturdy. It must have withstood hundreds of storms and blizzards. I stood with my back against its trunk, bent my head back, and looked up. It seemed to reach into the sky. I felt its rough bark. It even smelled ancient. I wondered what it would be like to be a tree and stand so still and so quiet for so long. So much was happening around that tree, yet it seemed not to notice.

They all find a big tree they think might be the one E.M. found. Some trees have several people around them, others have only one or two. Martin checks out some of them to see if they really do smell ancient and seem to reach into the sky. Not everyone agrees on which tree is the one E.M. found, but each person finds one that matches the description. Martin brings them back together again to read the eighth entry:

I wanted to cross the stream, so I looked for a good spot. I thought about trying to cross over on a tree that had fallen completely across it, but I decided it might be better to try a rocky area a little way downstream.

The group finds both the fallen tree and the crossing area. They cross over on the rocks, Martin giving a hand to those who are a bit shaky. When they have all crossed over successfully (with the exception of a few wet feet), they get in a circle and check where they are on their maps, as Martin reads the ninth entry:

I found an old trail going along the side of the stream, so I followed it a ways. I soon came to an area where the gurgling sound of the stream was especially loud. What a great "Listening Post"!

The group follows the trail until they find a good place to listen to the creek. Martin asks everyone to find a comfortable spot and sit very quietly as he reads the next entry:

I sat very still at my Listening Post and closed my eyes so I could concentrate on listening... Some sounds were very faint, so I cupped my hands behind my ears and pointed them toward what I wanted to hear. I didn't think about what was making each sound; I concentrated on the sound itself. I even tried to imitate some of the sounds in my head using letters of the alphabet.

After a few minutes of listening (and explaining more about tuning into the sounds themselves), Martin gets the group back together to read the next to the last entry.

I continued walking down along the stream until I came to a big bend. I wanted to cross the stream again, so I found a good spot with some rocks near a very large fallen tree.

When they have found the spot and crossed over the stream, Martin gets them back in a circle again. *"Look at the map; we're almost back where we started,"* observes one participant.

"I think you're right," Martin agrees. "In fact, this next passage is the last one in the diary." He reads the twelfth entry:

I found a big feather lying on the gravel next to the stream. When I picked it up, I noticed that it was clean; it must have come off a bird very recently. I carried it with me as I followed a path up to the bottom of a little hill. There I noticed a tree off to the left, part way up the hill, that had a small, cave-like hole hollowed out of its base. I still had my nut from the Miniature World as well as my feather, so I decided to put them both into this hiding place. Maybe they will still be there when I go back again someday!

"I see where E.M. must have put them," someone shouts.

"It must be in that tree right over there." They head over to take a look, and, sure enough, tucked away inside the hole are a feather and a nut. The feather looks a bit old and worn, and the nut looks like it has been chewed on, but it must be the right spot. Martin suggests that they leave the special objects they found in the Miniature World in there for E.M. to find, too. Maybe they will also come back here one day and find them as well!

At the top of the hill, they see the spot where they began. *"Yea, we did it!"*

They were able to use E.M.'s diary and map to follow E.M.'s footsteps and have an adventure of their own as they discovered this new place few people know.

General Notes – "E.M.'s Diary"

1. The key to making this structured activity seem unstructured is having a map that corresponds well to the diary entries and the actual site. The participants should be able to follow the map and diary without the necessity of having you continually steer them on to the right course.

2. The actual order of the pages and the specific wording in the diary will have to fit your activity site. Here are some important things to keep in mind when selecting a site:
   - find an area that is not heavily used and that the kids will not have been in before
   - put in some adventurous things to do, like crossing a stream on a log, rocks, or rope bridge

3. This is an active, exciting experience, and, especially with a large group, you need to use things like the timing and pace of the entry readings, and references you make to the map, to keep the group together and on track. Be sure to have the group get in a circle for each entry reading.

4. Let the participants lead the way in following the map, but have the leader read the diary entries to make sure everyone

can hear and has time to do the things the diary suggests. Don't forget to share a few natural history tidbits about some of the participants' discoveries.

5. On the large map of the Earthkeepers Training Centre that arrives in the classroom before the trip, indicate the area of E.M.'s Diary but don't label it that, just mark it as an unexplored area or leave it as a noticeably blank spot on the map.

6. This activity is written to be part of the Earthkeepers program but it can also be done separately; simply substitute another character for E.M.

Cue Card – "E.M.'s Diary"

1. Ask if they would like to use E.M.'s Diary to explore an area hardly anyone ever goes into

2. Show the map – pass out a copy to each group of two or three

3. Explain procedures – you will read a diary entry, they will use the map to follow the entry

4. Head off to the start of the area, circle up, read the first entry, let them lead the way

5. For each entry, circle up: you read, they lead

6. Conclude in a circle where you began

Prop List - "E.M.'s Diary"

o 1 diary – old looking, with handwritten pages (in E.M.'s handwriting). Be sure to include more pages than the ones you are using so it will appear as if this is just one of E.M.'s many outings.

o 1 large map – rolled up parchment paper – it should be specific enough that the participants can use it along with the diary entries to find their way. It should have some definite landmarks and places, like the hiding spot and any stream crossings, but leave some things like "E.M.'s favorite tree" up to each participant to find within a certain area.

o 1 small copy of the map for each group of two or three participants

o 1 magnifying lens per participant

o 1 large feather and 1 nut for the hiding place

o 1 old, gnarled walking staff with E.M. carved into it; leave it leaning against a tree somewhere along the route.

○ 1 old bottle with a note from E.M. inside – place along the route in a spot where someone will find it. The note should read:

"Ah, you've found it! You must be pretty sharp if you found this. Only the sharpest observers will spot it.

I'm glad you're getting a chance to explore this little known area.

Is it as much of an adventure for you as it was for me?

Enjoy Yourselves,"

E.M.

"E" - Immersing Experiences
"Activities Encouraging Total Sensory Involvement"

Another vehicle essential to the Earthkeepers program is the Immersing Experience. We believe that in order to build a deep, caring relationship with the earth, it is necessary to have lots of rich, first-hand contact with it. An Immersing Experience provides an opportunity to break through some of the barriers that prevent many learners from getting more in touch with the natural world. These activities bring the senses to the fore-ground, giving a new and different perspective to a perhaps already familiar setting. We like to say an Immersing Experience makes the familiar unfamiliar by changing the participants' vantage point.

Imagine a group's delight when they arrive for an activity called SEASONS and are greeted by their trainer, now trans-formed into a film director. All the props are there: beret, direc-tor's chair, even a script for the play that's about to be filmed.

The kids are eager, but a little apprehensive when the direc-tor informs them that they are the actors in this production. E.M.'s experience with this season has been documented in a script that brings all the sights, sounds, smells and sensations of winter to life. The kids learn that they will take turns recreat-ing this season for each other. First, as the performers, they will act out E.M.'s experiences for a blindfolded audience of one. Then for the second act of the play, they will switch places and don the blindfolds to become the audience themselves.

First, the kids are reassured that they will have no lines to read. Only the director will read the script, and he demonstrates for them what he will expect them to do. As he reads along, there will be specific cues included. The kids will have a list of these cues, each one followed by instructions for what action to perform. For example, when the director reads, "The rotten log smells wonderful..." the performer will pick up a piece of a rotting log from his individual prop tray and hold it under the nose of his blindfolded partner.

Questions about the props are next and the director shows them exactly how, with the help of their prop managers (Guar-dians), and a little preparation time, they can each prepare a prop tray obtaining their needs from a large prop box and the surrounding woods. All the instructions and cues are readily available.

Once all the preparations are made and the giggling dies down, the director calls for action and the play is underway. It's hard to tell who has a better time – the exuberant performers or the willing audience. It's a great way for them to express their enthusiasm over touching and smelling and listening without feeling self-conscious. Viva the play!

"Seasons"

"Have any of you ever been performers in a play?" Laurie, wearing sunglasses and a beret, asks. Hands shoot up throughout the group. "How many of you have ever been in the audience for a play?" Laurie then asks. More hands go up. "Great!" exclaims Laurie. "Quite an experienced group we have here. In just a minute you will get to be both performers and audience for a special play called 'Seasons' in our Woodland Theatre."

A few worried glances prompt Laurie to allay some concerns. "You don't have to worry if you are a bit shy about performing in front of a large audience, because you will be performing for just one person." Laurie pauses while the group wonders about this strange remark. "And furthermore, that person will be blindfolded," she adds. "And you don't have to start panicking because you have to memorize lots of lines; you don't have any lines at all." The group is really buzzing now. "As you can tell, this play is going to be a bit different; I'd better explain how it works."

"You are going to recreate for another person, using sounds and smells and touches, what makes up a day like today. I have two stories, each describing how E.M. explored the area outside on a day like this. Half of you will be performing one story while the other half is your audience (it's one on one, but all at the same time). Then you will switch roles; those of you who were the performers for the first story, Act I, will be the audience for the second story, Act II. In other words, the Act I audience will become the Act II performers."

"As Director of the Woodland Theatre, I will be reading the stories out loud, while each performer will help his or her audience, who is blindfolded, experience the smells and sounds and touches that I am describing in the story. For instance, if I am telling about how rough the bark of a tree feels, each performer might have a piece of bark for his or her audience to feel.

"First, I have a copy of the story you will be performing for you to look over. Read it carefully so you will know what kinds of things you will be helping your audience experience." Laurie divides the group into two crews and passes out a copy of the Act I story to the Act I performers and a copy of the Act II story to each of the Act II performers. When they have finished reading to themselves, Laurie continues, "Notice the prop lists at the bottom of the story sheet. The list labelled 'Prop Box' tells what items are available in our prop box over here. The list labelled 'off-stage' gives you some ideas on the kinds of things you might want to gather outdoors. Right now we're going to head out to do some prop gathering and experience for ourselves what this day is like. When we return, you can visit the prop box and rehearse for a few minutes before the performance begins."

Laurie hands a tray to each person to use to hold the things they gather, and they head outside, each crew to a slightly different part of the forest so they don't see what the other group is gathering. Everyone finds the things on the list and some other things as well. When all are finished, Laurie asks them to cover up their props with a piece of cloth and come inside. Indoors, each crew has a separate area to practice in. They go to their own prop box to get their final props and then practice using them with other members of their group.

When both crews are ready, Laurie takes Act II performers into the Woodland Theatre and has them sit on the floor in a circle with their backs toward the center. They each put their covered trays of props behind their back. Laurie then passes out the blindfolds. When all are fully blindfolded and silent, Laurie leads the Act I performers in and seats each person opposite and facing a blindfolded Act II performer. (Act I performers get their props ready while Laurie introduces the play.)

"Welcome to the Woodland Theatre. The play today is 'Seasons – A Cold, Wintery Day', by E.M. It is the story of a person exploring the forest on a day much like today." Laurie pauses, then begins, "It's a crisp, cold wintery day. Everything seems so still and lifeless, but I notice a patch of green around the base of a tree and reach down to feel a soft green carpet of moss." The Act I performers have their audience feel a piece of moss. "It even smells like spring!" They hold it up to their audience's nose.

Laurie continues with Act I, and the performers continue to help their audience hear and smell and feel the wintery day being described. When the story is finished, Laurie asks the audience to give the performers a hand. He then reminds the audience to keep the blindfolds on while the performers put their props back on their trays and put the covered trays behind their backs. The blindfolds then come off and are given to the Act II performers to wear – amid surprises and exclamations as the audience finds out who their performers were.

When everyone in the new audience has a blindfold and the Act II performers have their props ready (no one had to exchange seats), Laurie begins Act II. "Silence on the set, please. 'Seasons – A Cold, Wintery Day' – Act II. A cold wind blows against my face..."

At the end of Act II, the audience gives the performers a hand and the performers hide their props on their trays before the audience takes off the blindfolds. Each crew goes back to their rehearsal area to return their props to the prop box and the forest. When the groups get back together, Laurie thanks them for doing such a wonderful job of recreating this season of the year. They not only helped another person experience it more fully, they experienced it in new ways themselves as they gathered their props.

General Notes – "Seasons"

1. Two beginning stories for a winter's day are included. You will need to write your own stories for other seasons or conditions. The two stories you use for the two acts should both describe the same day but should emphasize different ways of exploring its different sounds and smells and textures.

2. While it is important to give some suggestions for props to gather and what to do with them, it is also important to let the participants use their own ideas on what to use at differ-

ent points in the story.

3. When you are using this activity in the Earthkeepers program, have the two prop boxes locked with an 'E' key so the participants can use their Experience key to open the box, thus using their experience to help recreate an experience for another person.

Cue Card – "Seasons"

1. Ask – ever been a performer? Audience?
2. Don't worry – audience of one, blindfolded, no lines
3. Explain play – recreate smells, sounds, touches of a day like today for someone
4. Split group in two – pass out stories, let them read
5. Gather props outside
6. Get props from box and let them rehearse
7. Seat Act II performers – in a circle, facing out, props behind back, blindfolds on
8. Seat Act I performers – each opposite and facing one Act II performer
9. Read Act I story
10. Applaud, cover and put props behind back, remove blindfolds (switch blindfolds – not places)
11. Read Act II story
12. Applaud, cover props, remove blindfolds
13. Groups return to rehearsal area and return props
14. Thank everyone for a great performance

Prop List – "Seasons"

o 1 Director's outfit – sunglasses, beret, maybe a director's chair
o 1 copy per participant of the appropriate story with suggested props
o 1 cloth-covered tray per participant – to hold props
o 2 prop boxes, one for Act I props and one for Act II props
o Props for the prop boxes – from the list for each story – 1 per participant
o 1 blindfold per two participants

Script – "Seasons"

A Cold Wintery Day – Act I

(Brief Sample)

It's a crisp, cold wintery day. Everything seems so still and lifeless. But I notice a patch of green at the base of a tree and reach down to feel a soft carpet of moss. It even smells like spring!

I sit very still for a moment and listen to the silence of the winter forest. It's not quite silent, though. I hear a faint gurgling sound in the distance. I head toward the sound and discover a stream. Much of it is frozen over with a layer of ice that feels slick and cold when I touch it.

Part of the stream is open where the water pours over the rocks, making that gurgling sound. I put my finger into the icy water, but just for a second.

As I step back into the forest I find a spot where a squirrel has dug up a supply of nuts. I reach down through the dead leaves and pull out an acorn. It feels and smells sort of strange, probably from being in the soil since fall. I wonder if this one will make it through the winter to grow into a new young tree in the spring?

Suggested Props – Act I

Prop Box:
> water in container – shake for gurgling sound and feel for icy water

Gather Outside:
> small piece of moss – feel and smell
> dead leaves – feel and smell
> acorn – feel and smell
> other items determined by the performer

A Cold, Wintery Day – Act II
(Brief Sample)

The cold wind blows against my face as I step into the forest. I stand still for a moment and listen to the sound of it rustling the few dead leaves that are still clinging to the branches. The wind dies down and all is silent. Just then I hear the tap-tap-tap sound of a bird searching for a meal in a dead branch.

Later, I bend down and brush away some snow to find out what's beneath. I feel the dead leaves that cover the soil. They even have a good smell when I crunch them up.

I reach down and touch the frozen soil. It's hard to believe that this rock-hard ground will soften up enough in the spring for tiny new plants to push up through it.

When I stand back up, I notice a small twig on a tree right in front of me. I feel the bud on its tip. Even in the midst of all this cold, the tree is getting ready to open its leaves in the sun when springtime arrives.

Suggested Props – Act II

Prop Box:
>   index card – fan for wind
>   frozen soil – feel and smell

Gather Outside:
>   dead leaves – feel and smell and shake for rustling sound
>   dead sticks – to hit together for "tapping" sound
>   twig with buds – feel
>   other items determined by the performer

CHAPTER
F I V E

THE LEADERSHIP GUIDELINES

The following guidelines for Earthkeepers leaders are the result of many years of observing both leaders and learners in the environmental education field. During this time we have learned a great deal ourselves about setting goals, motivating learners, and assuring full participation. Through our observations and study, plus numerous trial and error pilots, a number of insights about outdoor learning have evolved. In this brief section we cannot spell out all of our guidelines in detail, but we have tried to include the most important aspects. Each of the activity sources cited here includes important information for the leaders who use them, and each activity includes its own "general notes" for its leaders. Sunship Earth also contains an entire chapter on our general approach to learning. However, we can reiterate here some "uncommon" things to do when conducting our activities, and some "common" things to avoid.

Things To Do:

1. CREATE MAGICAL LEARNING ADVENTURES

   Remember: We want to pull our learners, not push them.

   To be honest, it's going to take a special effort on your part to create the atmosphere necessary for this program. We have done a lot of the groundwork for you in the way the activities are set up, but much of their success will depend on the special feeling you contribute. You are the all-important catalyst for making the program synergistic, for assuring that it becomes more than just the sum of its parts. Please don't be reluctant to let go a bit, to let the activities pull you along as well as your learners, but then don't add much more "magic" either. We don't want the magic to overwhelm the message. Like a good artist you will have to make sure all the ingredients work together to produce the intended result. Most important: be sure to establish an atmosphere right from the start to convey the feeling that these activities are part of an adventure, an adventure that you and your learners are embarking on together.

2. FOCUS ON SHARING AND DOING

Remember: It's not what you tell them that's important, but what they do with what you tell them.

So it's going to be critical for you to keep the focus on the doing and support the whole effort with the feeling that you are taking on a role in order to share a special experience with your learners. Try to resist that urge to show your participants everything about what's happening. Instead, let the activity itself provide the leadership and pull you and your learners along in discovering and sharing the intended messages together. It's no mystery that we learn best through experience. So we want to avoid that old game of show and tell and replace it with share and do. We can all probably remember sitting and listening to someone telling us how to do something and thinking, "Gosh, that sounds easy," but when we got home and tried it we didn't know where to start. We missed the experience of doing it ourselves and thus missed much of the learning.

3. EMPHASIZE THE 3 R'S: REWARD, REINFORCE, RELATE

Remember: You get the behaviour you reward for.

Catch them doing something good and give them a pat on the back. Reinforce the main points by repeating them over and over. That's the fourth R – repetition. Much of a good learning experience takes place after the activity.

Remember: It's what you can do with what you do that counts.

When they're not doing the activities, ask them at every opportunity to do something with what they've done. And be sure to help them relate the point of each activity to their own lives. We want them to see how they are a part of these systems, how their actions each day are governed by and impact upon the ecological processes of life.

4. MODEL POSITIVE ENVIRONMENTAL BEHAVIOURS

Remember: They'll recall what they saw you do long after they have forgotten what you said.

Look for ways you can demonstrate good environmental habits yourself. In the end, the students will probably remember some of your personal habits long after they've forgotten whatever you had to say. If you can come across a bit "larger than life" to them, and at the same time demonstrate some sound environmental behaviours that they can easily adopt, then your place in their memory-bank of influential leaders is assured. (For ideas, consider what you wear, tools you carry, what you eat and drink and how it's packaged, simple actions like stopping to smell a flower or making sure the "energy-leaking" lights are off. Above all, put a sparkle in your eye and a spring in your step!) Be careful though that you don't make yourself the message. Lots of programs in our field confuse their means with their ends.

Things to Avoid:

1. NAMING AND LABELING

Remember: Naming is not knowing.

Stick to the names for broad categories of things. Most of the others just get in the way. We believe it's more important to focus on the processes of life than its pieces. In fact, if you stop and think about it, names are really like landmarks; you just don't need very many of them to find your way. And let's stop repeating those same tired old methods of the past. We think it's a tragedy that most people in our societies can name a few trees and birds and such, but cannot explain the flow of sunlight energy that supports the life of our planet. While we use some names of things in our Earthkeepers activities, for the most part, we either play down their importance or use names that will encourage a different perception of something. Always go for the broadest category possible: a night-flying, insect-eating mammal is far preferable to a Pipistrellus subflavus, and just a bat is much better than an Eastern Pipistrelle.

2. TALKING WITHOUT A FOCAL POINT

Remember: Most people are visual learners.

They need to see something to help them make it more concrete. Talking without a focal point is like learning to swim without water. You could still do it, but why make it so hard on everyone? In these activities, we've tried to make sure there's a focal point whenever the leader is talking. If you find yourself rattling on without something for the learners to look at, chances are good you've begun ad-libbing. It's important that you keep the pace of these activities fairly brisk, and keep your comments fairly limited.

3. PLAYING TWENTY QUESTIONS

Remember: The activity should do the teaching, not the teacher.

We believe the task of the teacher is to set up and guide the learners in exciting learning situations. And most of the doing should be for the kids, not the leader. Quizzing the kids to work them around to your answer means that you're probably doing most of the doing yourself. Perhaps that's the source of that old adage: "The best way to learn something is to teach it." No wonder, the teachers were doing most of the doing! Frankly, "Twenty Questions" represents a poor substitute for good doing. Lots of learners don't play, and a few articulate kids usually dominate the action. Let's make the task the "teacher," and the teacher the guide.

To be honest this is one of the most difficult of our guidelines to follow. Lots of weak educational activities in this field depend upon the leader to make them do their job afterwards (usually under the guise of "discussion"). We want the point of our learning experiences to be more self-evident for a larger percentage of the participants. And we don't want to risk losing many of the kids because the leaders constantly play the "Twenty Questions" game with them.

Be sure to explain this to your volunteer helpers as well. It's one thing to help the learners relate things to their daily lives, but it's quite another to set up a pressurized atmosphere that destroys the enthusiasm for learning that we're trying so hard to create.

In this field learning "discussions" are definitely our most overworked educational tool and may be our most dangerous. Since kids' imitative abilities are pretty well-honed by this age, you can be easily misled in a discussion into thinking that they really are taking away dozens of ecological understandings from a fairly simple activity. It's most likely untrue. Besides, a primary reason why we forget an estimated 90% of what we learn in school is probably because such a large amount of what we supposedly absorbed took place in discussions that were not well-grounded in relevant concrete actions. If we're going to go to all the trouble to take a class outside to begin with, let's not spend our time out there conversing with a few kids.

4. DRIFTING INTO ACTIVITY ENTROPY

Remember: Pay attention to the details.

All the props and roles and techniques serve as tools to help you do the job. A craftsman with no tools is going to have a tough time building anything. Don't carelessly throw away the smallest item until you're sure you have a thorough grasp of your job and your product.

Remember: The first rule of tinkering is to save all the parts.

It's easy to decide to eliminate some of the props or change some of the roles in our activities, rationalizing that they are not really crucial to the activity – or to make do with an inadequate prop when a little more effort would produce a really good tool. Of course, no one can say at exactly what point an activity will be so diminished by one of the changes that it will cease to do its job. Energetic leaders can get away with a lot, even if it means they burn out sooner themselves.

We believe the props and roles utilized in our activities are integral parts, chosen for their ability to intensify and sharpen the learning experiences. Please be sensitive to all the little details, and let the program work for you. We think you'll be pleasantly surprised at the results.

APPENDIX "A"

Excerpts from the "Y" Tasks Flyer

Dear Parents,

As part of the Earthkeepers program, your child has earned two keys – a **K** (knowledge) key representing the knowledge learned at the Earthkeepers Training Centre and an **E** (experience) key representing experiences in the natural world.

To earn the third key, **Y** (yourself), your child must do four tasks. The first two tasks are ways of lessening his or her impact on the natural world by using less energy and materials. Your child has chosen one way of using less energy and one way of using less materials. To earn the **Y** key, these need to become habits, something that is done regularly. When your child has done them consistently for at least one month, please sign on the next page.

The next two tasks are ways of getting closer to nature by experiencing it first hand. Your child has chosen two tasks to deepen his or her feelings for the natural world. When they are completed, please sign the bottom of the last page.

When your child has completed all four tasks and you have signed both pages, this leaflet can be taken back to school and your child will receive a **Y** key and can open the **Y** box to find out the third secret meaning of E.M.

Thank you very much for your help.

E.M.

LESSENING IMPACT TASKS

ENERGY - CHOOSE ONE:

☐ **Heat. . .**
When you feel cold, put on a sweater rather than turn up the heat.

☐ **Electricity. . .**
When you are not using a room, make sure all lights and appliances are turned off.

☐ **Transportation. . .**
Instead of getting a ride in a car to somewhere you often go, begin walking or riding your bike.

MATERIALS - CHOOSE ONE:

☐ **Water. . .**
When you are using water to wash your hands or brush your teeth, turn the faucet on gently, and leave it running only as long as you need it.

☐ **Paper. . .**
Write on the back of writing paper instead of throwing it away.

☐ **Aluminum. . .**
Recycle all the aluminum you use.

My son/daughter has done the tasks checked above consistently for at least one month. I believe they have become habits he/she will continue.

_____   _____
          Parent's Signature   Date

DEEPENING FEELINGS TASKS

CHOOSE TWO:

☐ **Magic Spot. . .**
Find a magic spot near your home and spend time there at least once a week for a month. Remember that a Magic Spot is in a natural area away from human buildings and activity. It is a place where you can sit quietly alone and think about your Earthkeeper training and use all your senses to get to know your spot.

☐ **Explorations. . .**
Find a new natural area to explore. Spend at least two hours getting "immersed" in it – finding "miniature worlds," listening to new sounds, and discovering natural treasures – on two different visits.

☐ **Diaries. . .**
Continue writing in your Earthkeeper diary while at your Magic Spot or while exploring a natural area at least once a week for a month. Write down your thoughts on your tasks, new natural places you've visited, or neat discoveries you've made.

☐ **Records. . .**
Write four stories or poems, one each week, about your Earthkeepers training, a natural area you explore, or your Magic Spot. You may want to share your stories or poems with other Earthkeepers at school.

My son/daughter has done the tasks checked above to experience the natural world.

_____   _____
Parent's Signature   Date

Dear Parents,

As part of the Earthkeepers program, your child has earned a **K** (knowledge) key and an **E** (experience) key at the Earthkeepers Training Centre and has tasks to do to earn the **Y** (yourself) key. The final key is the **S** (sharing) key.

To earn an **S** key, your child must share his/her knowledge and experiences with another person – a friend, a brother or sister, or you. Your child has chosen two knowledge tasks and two experience tasks to share. Your child's teacher has specific information on how to do the knowledge tasks, and the experience tasks are described on the next page.

When all four tasks have been shared, please sign the bottom of the last page. This leaflet can then be taken back to school, and your child will receive an **S** key and can open the **S** box to find out the fourth secret meaning of E.M. He/she will then be an Earthkeeper – Level I.

Thanks for all your support and encouragement.

E.M.

SHARING EXPERIENCES

SOLITUDE: Magic Spot
Help someone find their own Magic Spot. Be sure it is a natural area away from human buildings and activity. Tell them to sit quietly and alone for at least 15 minutes. They should use their senses to get to know their spot.

DISCOVERY: Map and Diary
Introduce someone to a new natural area by making a map and diary for them to use in exploring it. Keep in mind how you followed E.M.'s diary and map. Be sure to note miniature worlds, listening posts, and other special places.

OBSERVATION: Sensory Walk
Take someone on a walk in a natural area and help them use all of their senses to enjoy its natural wonders. Have them sit very quietly with eyes closed and listen to the sounds. Have them find things that feel rough, smooth, sharp, dull, hard, and soft. Let them find the strongest smell they can, then the sweetest. They should use their eyes to see what is the farthest away, the tiniest thing, and the most colourful. You'll probably have some other ideas for things they can do.

IMMERSION: Recreating A Season
Write a story about exploring a natural area. Describe things you heard, felt, or smelled. Read it to another person who is blindfolded. Use props that you have gathered to help the person smell, feel, and hear the things you are describing in the story. Try to make someone feel like he or she is really there.

SHARING

ACTIVITY I SHARED   **WHO I SHARED IT WITH**

Knowledge – Choose Two:

☐ **Energy Flow**
Munch Line Monitor _____

☐ **Cycling**
Speck Trail _____

☐ **Interrelationships**
Connector Inspector _____

☐ **Change**
Time Capsule _____

Experience – Choose Two:

☐ **Solitude**
Magic Spot _____

☐ **Discovery**
Map and Diary _____

☐ **Observation**
Sensory Walk _____

☐ **Immersion**
Recreating a Season _____

My son/daughter has shared the four activities checked above with other people.

_____   _____
Parent's Signature   Date

INDEX